COMING HOME

written by **Naomi Kilbreth**

AngryEaglePublishing.com

Printed in the United States of America

First Printing, 2021

ISBN 978-1-7366043-4-2

No techniques are recommended without
proper instruction or safety measures and
training. The author nor publisher
assumes no liability for any action
presumed from this book.

Editorial, and formatting provided
through Angry Eagle Publishing.
Images obtained with license stock
photos or public domain.
Cover Image Naomi Kilbreth
Cover by Dauntless Cover Design

Dedication

To wild souls everywhere in search of adventure.

Six people, a tiny camper, and an adventure

to freedom

COMING HOME

Introduction

Snowflakes fall gently to the ground, adding to the already deep drifts in the valley. The woods are deep, dark, and still. Pine trees bear the only signs of life, as all creatures hide away in their holes to keep warm and dry through the cold, harsh winter. A few brave pioneers await the end of the winter season in their tiny cabins throughout the unclaimed territory, including John Greenwood, who would one day become the namesake of this little hill, and Alexander Shephard, who would soon become the unofficial mayor of this expanse of uncharted land in an exchange with this Massachusetts colony for his cartography skills. Like every other pioneer in the north, they stocked their wood stoves and remained hunkered down for the winter. Yet, in this unlikely time, two travelers arrived after a week-long journey by horse and wagon, with all their belongings, and a baby nearly due to be born.

What was it that drove this newly wedded couple to move to this practically unexplored land, 150 miles away from family, with the birth of their first child nearly upon them? And in the middle of winter no less, where housing and employment, or a ready piece of land to farm were not guaranteed? Could it have been that their unplanned pregnancy was an embarrassment to the family? Were they excited by the prospect of starting their life together in a new place? Or were they perhaps attempting to escape the ravages of the war being fought to the south? The gravestones with their names and dates will never spill their secrets and leave much to the imagination.

This very couple, 24-year-old Zacheus Rowe and 18-year-old Bethiah Day Rowe, moved from Gloucester, Massachusetts to Hebron, Maine in the winter of 1774-75, although it wouldn't possess that town name until 1792, and remained the property of Massachusetts until 1820. They built a homestead, complete with a large cornfield on the ledge-covered hillside, as the story goes, and had another nine children together after their first was born that undoubtedly rocky winter.

Years pass. Newly established governments divide the land, the war ends, a state unifies, and more travelers arrive. Children are born, parents die, and the generations continue. Properties are purchased and sold, homes are constructed, farms developed, and prosperous businesses are established. Despite all of the changes to the landscape, 20 acres of the original land, in the little town of Hebron, remained in the Rowe family. Seven times it was passed down after that adventurous duo embarked on a quest for a new life, and that's where our story begins.

If not for the bushes and trees blocking our view, we would still be able to see the corner of the lot where what could be the stone foundation of my husband Glen's sixth great-grandparents home still lay, crumbled, and partially buried by the earth as it heals. A few unmarked stones nearby tell the tale of ancestors' past. It is strange to think that this land was inhabited just a couple of generations back by the same Rowe family and that we, an unremarkable family with a modest four children, have the honor of carrying on their homesteading blood today. And is it simply ironic that we would also unintentionally share their wedding date?

Adventures are incredibly easy to live through other people. In fact, as a society, America has gotten so used to experiencing the feel-good emotions that come with watching such things on TV, reading about them in books, and following them on social media, that we hardly know what an adventure actually feels like for ourselves. As Aesop said, *"It's easier to be brave from a safe distance."* A brave few will hike a big mountain, set out on a quest, or start fresh in a new place; all relatable adventures that a support system is almost always available for. Perhaps the most relatable adventure is raising a family, but even this generally includes a support system to help you along the way. A true adventure is one in which you yourself step foot out the door, having no idea exactly what lies ahead. This is where we found ourselves on May 4, 2011; stepping out on a six-year adventure with many twists and turns.

9

Author John Eldredge wrote, *"Adventure, with all its requisite danger and wildness, is a deeply spiritual longing written into the soul of man."* Truth be told, we knew that adventure was a part of us, long before we had plans to start a homestead, or were given any motivating reason to move off grid. Somehow, that thirst for thrilling escapades was passed down from Zacheous Rowe, and it was going to find it's expression through Glen; starting this new life was simply the outpouring of these deep roots. And really, what is life without some adventure, a few daring escapades; some thrill to push one to the edge, beyond what was assumed to be the limits of reasonable excitement?

In fact, it is the day-in-day-out mundane; of going to work, paying the bills, mowing the lawn, being entertained, that has so many screaming, "What the hell is the point of it all?!" With bills and debts piled high, and no hope of escape. Parents unable to play with the kids because they are too busy, and kids confined to a fenced-in tarmac to play. Does it really surprise us that a growing number of families are saying, "Screw it" to the limits and doing their own thing? You'd have to be living in a hole in the ground not to see all the media reports popping up of tent cities, tiny house builders, and camper dwellers. Look up campers for sale on yard sale type forums and you'll see loads of people talking about how they're in the market for a camper to live in, in the hopes that an escape from "normal" will give them the freedom and adventure they seek.

A new generation has arisen, of people sick of the false hope of a cute little cape with two-car garage and white picket fence, and high end, debt-ridden, college-earned careers enabling two-week vacations to Disneyland with the kids. Folks, the reality is that many people who set off in search of this American lifestyle find themselves over their heads, short of the mark, and scrambling to get out of the rat race, but it takes guts to dare to jump ship. A visionary like Glen seems always ready for the next adventure well before it's begun, but it's easier to examine what makes another person who they are. For myself, I am a complicated mix of enjoying life on the fringe and craving acceptance: I question the status quo, but I still need my tribe. I once read that to be the happy wife of a visionary you must be a little reckless and blind in one eye to enjoy the roller coaster ride that will be her new life. That may seem a bit extreme, but I laughed in recognition when I first read it and continue to feel it's relevance in my life today!

In these past nine years since we moved to the land, we have seen wonders and horrors, beauty, and ugliness. Just as a thru-hiker on the Appalachian will experience extreme depths in the intensity of the experience; pushing themselves to go further than they ever thought they could, and yet feeling extreme heights in the pride of their ability to pull themselves through those depths to the heights, this adventure has shown us amazing things we never would have experienced otherwise, but it has not been without its soul-shaking trials.

Despite all these wide swings from exhilaration to trauma, one of the most memorable things I have experienced here is the loneliness that comes with not experiencing it alongside a community. Glen and I have our deep partnership (and we wouldn't have survived out here otherwise), but when you debate sharing your feelings about your lifestyle with others because you know they can't relate, it adds weight to the pack. Then you add the misrepresentation given by reality TV, where people suddenly think they know how you live because they saw a twenty-minute episode glossing over the highlights, and now you wonder: why bother trying to explain myself? "We'll always be the outsiders, no matter how idolized the lifestyle is," you think. You fear most people will only attempt to live it through others, and thus also misunderstand everything your way of life represents.

It is from this place of loneliness, and the day-to-day struggle of routine in hardship that I had begun growing hard; burnt to the adventure; ready for a reprieve, and I hated that. People came to us and said, "how can we do this too?!" And I, making judgments about their readiness and the harsh realities I knew they'd face, would respond (half-jokingly), "Easy! Don't!"

Yet while the reality-TV perspective leaves people with a false, unrealistic view of our chosen life, I know this is no fault of their own. What reason should anyone have for understanding the truth unless they have experienced it? They don't know anything unless it's included in such a show. This book is my attempt to set the record straight and to encourage you to have your own adventures.

You need to know the truth. You deserve the truth. I want you to know why we didn't give up when things got rough; what kept us going. I want you to know what we missed out on by not leaping sooner; what we treasure from this experience. I want you to know how we really live; in case you are considering stepping out on an adventure and spreading your wings. And perhaps, in the process, those who are living adventures for other people won't feel so alone. Perhaps, those who are living adventures through other people will understand a little better. And hopefully, my own heart will continue to be softened, so the memories of this experience will hold a more treasured place in my heart.

I am going to be real with you. I did not intend to write this book. As far as I was concerned, once the journey was over, I didn't want to relive it. But I am a writer. This story welled up inside me so that I could feel it more than think it: the memories of laughter and tears, and shouts of joy and grief, all rolled up in a ball in my gut. It wanted to come out. The truth of the experience demanded to be expressed. It demanded to be told.

This book is our personal experience; our truth, our memoir. Others who have walked similar paths may have viewed things from another angle, another perspective, and that's okay. And as with all memoirs, memory can play funny tricks, so I'll just preface this by saying that this book's purpose is not to give a precise history, but to share our story; to show you in the way words do, what it was like for one average family to take the leap; to jump ship and create the life they wanted. We wanted. We did leap. We intentionally created our life. This is our story.

Be understanding. Be inspired. Be adventurous.

Chapter One

~Brave~

It's quiet. Almost eerily so. The air is still, and all I can hear is the sound of the clock.

Tick. Tick. Tick. Tick.

It's late; I don't know what time it is, and I don't feel like getting up to see. We must be in the new moon because it is pitch black. I never noticed the dark like this before; it's so much different than our old home. We called it that after we moved: "our old home." It sat right on the edge of a side road, closer to action and streetlights. It wasn't even that big of a town, but it still felt more civilized than this. Out here, several hundred feet from the road, it felt so empty. There were no streetlights, and only the rare car driving by. I was left alone to my thoughts as my husband and three young children, not even school age yet, slept peacefully in our simple, tag-along camper.

Could we do this? Could we make it work? Could we make our dreams come true, and use only what we had to build a self-sufficient home, and not owe anyone a cent?

The sound of a whip-poor-will broke the silence nearby. This land had so much potential. There was plenty of space, privacy provided by the woods, open sky to help us power our home, and even the promise of water. Yes, we can do this.

Have you stopped to notice the abundance of stories about adventures? I enjoy collecting quotes about them. It inspires me; reminds me that we are on the right path. How about this famous statement by the character, Bilbo Baggins, speaking to his nephew, Frodo in The Lord of The Rings:

"It's a dangerous business, going out of your front door. You step onto the road, and if you don't keep your feet, there's no telling where you might be swept off to."

Of course, if you know the story, Bilbo was speaking from personal experience. He knew that if you get caught up by the spirit of adventure, any sort of story could unfold; considered quite a dangerous thing for a hobbit!

One cliché analogy used to explain the nature of an adventure is to tell about a ship setting sail. I know nothing about sailing, however. In fact, the biggest boats I have ever been on were ferries, in sight of land no-less. Somehow, using that analogy just doesn't feel relatable, so I'll stick with an analogy with which I am quite familiar:

having children.

When you set out on the journey of parenthood, it is easy to believe that you know enough to get started, and you're smart enough to figure out the rest along the way. While this is generally the case, some… okay, probably all of us, are tempted before starting the journey, to look smugly at people who have already become parents, thinking to ourselves that they are doing it wrong, which of course, we won't. We think that if we do A, B, then C, that all will go perfectly as planned, not considering that we might need more than a couple of backup plans along the way should anything take an unexpected turn.

And then your child is born. Isn't it funny how childbirth changes all that? I feel like just that experience alone, no matter how perfect and beautiful, shocks us into reality. We begin to realize that everything we thought we knew is worth shit, and if we're going to thrive through this adventure, it isn't so much knowledge we need, but the character to adapt and to put the knowledge into action, based on the situation at that moment. You can read all the books you want, but your kid is literally one in a million, and some days you will be riding high together, and other days it will take sheer will power and the grace of God to get you through.

We all know adventures are worth the having. Otherwise, the USA wouldn't exist as it is today, we wouldn't have cell phones, no one would be sent to space, and anyone daring to spend six months hiking the Appalachian trail would be looked at with disdain rather than awe; "why would you put yourself through that?!"

Whether we live the adventure ourselves or through someone else, we admire the tenacity, the strength, the courage pulled from some unknown inner place to draw the daring closer to their destination. It inspires us to greatness! It motivates us to live bravely and try new things, and it shapes our personality and polishes our character.

At some point, in the midst of an adventure being lived out, there is a moment of reckoning, where the adventurer, like the new parent, realizes they have to unlearn everything they thought they knew. This experience teaches us a valuable gift: to treasure the heart of those setting sail, and to be kind to oneself, for not understanding as much as we wish we had.

There is something beautiful and even mysterious about the heart of a new adventurer. We know their knowledge and experience is limited (any Disney movie will show you the character growth that happens during an adventure), but we also see an optimistic, courageous heart. They know not what lies ahead, but they choose to go anyway. They believe in the adventure. They trust in the learning process of the journey. It will shape them and mold them into maturity, like a potter forms a vase.

For now though, they are innocent, and joyful, if not a bit (or a lot) apprehensive. They see only potential for good, opportunity, and a clean slate. We can see this in other people, give them grace in the process, but can we give it to ourselves? Can we hold on to a bit of that innocent optimism and gratefulness for the process?

For my own journey, I moved from this place of optimism all

the way to resentment, but I am gratefully moving back toward the middle of the pendulum, to peace. This adventure has tried my soul in a way giving birth four times in five years did not. I wanted to give up along the way. I even tried to! But I'm glad we stuck it out because the thrill of reaching our goal, of accomplishing what we set out to do, of "placing our home within our house," as my grandmother said, was totally and completely worth every bit of it. Would I do it again? I'd rather not have to! Yet I am very content, happy to be where we are today, and that's good enough for me.

Just as Frodo's story began long before he left Hobbiton with Sam and the ring, our adventure had a back story as well.

December 9, 2010 was a Thursday afternoon like any other. Four-year-old Nemo and two-year-old Daphney were playing in the living room. Atlas, at nine months old, would have been taking a nap, and I was elbow deep in dishwater, cleaning up the kitchen so I could make dinner before Glen came home from work. The phone rang. It was Glen, no doubt calling me to chat on his way home; a not unusual routine. I propped the phone between my ear and shoulder and kept washing. "This is it," I paused mid-scrub. "I got the pink slip, and I finish out on Monday." I dried off my hands and stood at the counter in silence. All the preparations we had made in the past two years, the food storage, the alternative housing plans, and other prepping decisions, would not be uncalled for after all. All the concern about the economy, job security, the political scene, prepping and backup plans... it had all come to this moment.

For the previous year especially, we had been working hard to take precautions. Glen had been losing hours at work, because of major customers backing out on housing projects, stating that they wanted to wait and see what the stock market would do. The housing bubble had officially burst, and people were scared. Houses were being foreclosed on left and right, the unemployment rate was climbing steadily, and then one too many customers backed out and the last straw broke the camel's back. We were done.

If it had not been for all the preparations we had made, this would have been a dire situation. A lot of people in our position were not so fortunate. For the next five months, we lived comfortably in our house, paying our bills, and eating well, living off of savings, unemployment, stored firewood, and some of our food storage. If it were not for Glen suddenly being home all of the time, the kids would not have known anything had changed.

Between December 9, 2010, and our moving day, May 4, 2011, a lot of work needed to happen. We had to make some hard decisions, none of which were easy on the family, and we didn't take any of it lightly. Glen's dad wrote to us shortly after we announced our decision to give up the house and move off grid onto the land we were inheriting from them: "Mom and I would hate to see you make a decision that will affect your lives for years to come in response to a temporary situation of being unemployed," and proceeded to offer us a place to live in their home. My grandmother later said, "I doubt if I was happy to see any of you having to give up so much space to be crowded into such a small space… with your difficult money situation, I didn't see that there could be betterment within your lifestyle... I was sorry, yet still had a feeling of pride that you guys would challenge life as usual and 'live outside the box.'" My sister-in-law was less emotionally attached to our decision and provided an alternative point of view: "You and Glen, we always say, are an inventive couple, and dance to the beat of your own drum. The move wasn't a surprise since were close and you spoke of doing so, the struggle of mortgage payments, and wanting to live off grid. I think we were intrigued to watch and see how you would live, especially with littles in tow."

Jerry Minchey, author of The Truth About RV Living: The Good, The Bad, and The Ugly, along with several other books on RV living, had this to offer: "We would all like for our family and friends to agree with our decision and think we're making the right choice, but the truth is, they probably won't. Would your friends like the RV lifestyle? Probably not. At least most of them wouldn't. If they wouldn't like it for themselves, it's hard to imagine how they could be happy about you living this lifestyle. Don't worry about what they think about or about making them happy... It's your life. Go live it."

My sister-in-law continued: "Even though it's not a life we are living or wanted for ourselves, we surely commend you for doing so with four kids!" And that support was all we could hope for.

The land Zacheaus Rowe and his wife, Bethiah undoubtedly poured their souls into to transform into farmland, was passed down from son to son, until it came to his great great grandson, Solomon Rowe. Although it would continue to be passed down another two generations along the male lineage in the first half of the 20th century, it was one of Solomon's daughters who would later be known as Glen's great grandmother. After ownership of the land was passed down those last two generations, the youngest Rowe, Gard, moved out of state, and in his elder years he was ready to find a new Rowe descendant to take ownership of the family property. His daughters had little interest, so the land was divided into two lots, with almost half being sold to his cousin's daughter, Glen's mother, and her husband, on April 18, 2006, and the other lot was eventually sold to friends of ours in 2018, who also chose to live in a camper while they prepared to build a house. Now, we have the privilege of transforming this land back into a treasured home.

What if we hadn't inherited the land? Over the course of my blogging and book-writing, people have asked how to find land, and how to get approval to live off grid. I'm not sure how we would have handled our situation differently if this piece of the puzzle hadn't lined up like it did for us. We had certainly talked about buying land. We had heard Northern Maine was an excellent place for living under the radar, if not in near-complete seclusion. The greatest advice I would ever give when choosing land is to ask around. Ask people you know who live in towns you are interested in what it's like working with code enforcement, what leadership is like, and how the neighborhood is. The more opinions the better, but even if you have to resort to the reviews of strangers in a social media group, it will still give you information to help you decide where you would be happiest living.

Aside from the social and political climate of the area, you will of course also want to inspect the land for it's quality. If you are paying cash you will want to keep in mind basic questions like, how much land will you have to clear, fill in, or blast to put in a foundation? Is there sunlight for solar and gardens? Is there adequate privacy from the neighbors and the road, if that is your desire? However, all that said, there is one last piece of advice I would give you and that is, similar to family planning, don't wait until you are fully prepared, or you will never take the leap. Gather as much information as you need to make the best decision for you, and then be brave and do it.

Though getting the pink slip was a sudden turn of events, we had known that unemployment for him and many other Maine carpenters was likely, and we had been troubled by political and economic circumstances across our country, so we had already begun preparing for a worst-case scenario situation, the best that we could. After confirming in 2009 that our mortgage company was unwilling to assist us if our income should be temporarily put on hold, we made plans for an alternative living situation. Nearly a year before the day of the pink slip, we had purchased a small, old camper, and took it home to remodel. In the spring of 2010, we parked it on the land, built a little campsite around it, and spent as much time as we could there. We even planted a little garden, built a shed, and a water tower from which we could take gravity-fed showers from a five-gallon pail tied to a rope several feet over our heads. I remember celebrating our 6th wedding anniversary by sending the kids to the grandparents' and staying at our camp, staying up late into the night playing a board game Glen had designed, sharing lots of cuddles and giggles. Little did we know that less than a year later we would be living on that very plot of land.

That winter, after we decided to move, we began rearranging our lives, beginning with our home. We had a 1,600 square foot cape; an old house that in its original form had been the town's one room schoolhouse. Knowing that living in 200 square feet would be a shock to us all, we downsized ahead of time. We gave up living space in three rooms, and began using the dining room as the living room, the living room became the master bedroom, and the music room became the kids' bedroom. The upstairs and larger living room were shut off. We started taking shorter showers to practice water conservation, and packed up unused things, or stuff we wouldn't be able to use, for a yard sale we'd host on Memorial Day weekend at Glen's brother's. It was trendy at the time to play with the idea of minimalism. Many bloggers quoted the statement, "Keep only what you find useful or beautiful," but we minimized our belongings and space out of necessity to make our new lifestyle work.

Glen started building fencing that would go around our garden area, a solar dehydrator, and other things from recycled material we had on hand for our new home. By April, we purchased another camper, the one we would live in, brought it home using Papa's truck (newly outfitted with a special breaking system) and parked it in our driveway by the house. We painted, made curtains, replaced the flimsy table, rebuilt the bunk beds, added a baby gate to one of the beds, and otherwise began transforming this camper into our home. It was a 31' Dutchman, with no slide-outs, but it did have two bedrooms, one on either end. The only appliances it came with were the fridge and stove, but we had no intention of using a microwave anyway, which would have been a power hog. I remember giving tours to family and friends, feeling excited and motivated, but watching in curiosity, the expressions on their faces as they processed the fruition of our plans before their eyes.

Despite the abundant mud that spring, Glen began taking truckloads of belongings to the new land, parking by the road, and hauling it all across the field and up the hill in a sled or wagon, depending on that day's weather, to the original camper, which quickly turned into a storage unit. Our house became more and more empty. We built up excitement by making a paper chain with the kids, and each day they would take turns ripping off a loop, representing one less day to wait before the move.

The excitement of all the possibility ahead may have carried us through a season that would otherwise have been traumatic (Glen continued searching for jobs this whole time, with no luck), but each of us had to experience the grief of letting go. As expected, Nemo's time didn't come until several weeks after moving, and Glen's was in the days before the move. Mine came much earlier. We couldn't fit our crib into the camper of course, so I gave it to my cousin who was expecting her first baby; the crib all three of our babies had slept in. As I watched it be carried out the door, piece by piece, my heart ached. I thought to myself, "if I keep the crib, do I get to stay? Can everything stay the same?" But once it was gone, I was ready to move on. It was like closing one door and opening another.

The last day, May 4th, was a Wednesday. I don't remember why we chose to leave that day, other than understanding that we needed to go when the weather was sunny, which it was. No need to set up the camper in the rain. We rushed around taking care of this and that. Cleaning out one room at a time and making it off limits to the kids as we went.

We have a picture somewhere of Daphney, not yet three years old, sitting on a chair in our bedroom; the only thing left in the room. She was staring off into space. No doubt processing what was happening in her young mind the best that she could. We played hide and seek one last time. I mopped the kitchen floor, took one last look around, and closed the door.

I remember Papa, which is what we call Glen, pulling out of the driveway first, with the camper in tow, and the kids and I in the car behind him. We all waved goodbye to the house, and we were off.

"I don't know where this will go, but I will go 'with a spring in my step and smile on my face.' It will be an adventure with my favorite humans. We're in it together, and we're going to do something important and meaningful." I wrote this as an image of the feeling I had at the time, in an early draft of this book. Martin Luther King Jr. once made a statement that described this moment well: "You don't have to see the whole staircase. Just take the first step."

Boondocking is the term that most closely describes how we lived until we moved into our house. Docking brings us back to the sailing analogy; describing how a boat will come up alongside a dock, to park for a time. Boon refers to "the boonies." Whereas dry camping refers to setting up an RV where there are no hookups, boondocking involves camping in an undeveloped area. So called purists say it should also mean camping away from civilization in general, with no other human or dwelling in sight. This is of course the modern term. Before 1960, it was used in place of "parking" to refer to young people who would find a remote area to make out!

So boondocking it was. Little did we know that we would be living in our 31' camper for the next six years and two months, or about all the adventures we would have in the process.

Living off grid in a tiny home definitely has its advantages, beginning with all of the reasons people dream of moving out into the woods (Facebook memes, anyone?) and the freedom that comes with living on the road. For us though, full time RVing was never the end goal. It wasn't a solution to our mortgage problem, or the fruition of our homesteading dream. This move was simply the journey to our goal; the long road from one house to the next. From dependence to independence. From being stuck to being free. A six year long journey, beginning that beautiful Wednesday morning.

Our first stop was not to our land, 17 miles away, but Glen's parents', just a few miles before our destination. We parked the camper in their driveway and spent the first night there so that Glen could do a trial run of a few systems and fill up the water tank. In the meantime, I played around with organizing our things, and the kids, ran around outside and played with toys in their "toy area," which was actually the fourth bunk sans mattress. Everything felt so new and exciting, but also unsettled, since we hadn't finished our drive yet.

When we woke the next morning, Glen took a video of everyone for our YouTube channel, American Family Now. He asked four year old Nemo what he thought about our new home, and Nemo, having previously been very concerned about having enough room for his favorite toys, responded, "it doesn't look sad anymore."

On Thursday afternoon, we all drove to the land; Glen hauling the camper, and the kids in the car with me as before. The ground was still very soft, and it was getting late in the day by the time we arrived, so Glen settled on a temporary spot, a couple hundred feet from where we intended to set up camp, and we settled in for the night.

After that memorable first night on the land, the days sped by as they do. It was wonderful having Glen with us each day; one of the perks of being temporarily unemployed. We woke up together each day, and while the kids played we worked on various projects. Even though that spot we parked on was temporary, we still laid out a few old dock sections for a porch, set up the awning to collect rain water in a barrel, and built a small rock campfire pit. In those first few days, Glen also learned how to power the camper with our small solar system, though we also used a generator quite a bit. He also figured out how to refill the RV water tank using a 5 gallon bucket of water and a 12 volt pump with an RV filter, and of course, to begin composting the black water.

There were also farm chores to do. We had several chickens in the small coop Glen had driven over in the days before the move, and they needed a run to safely leave the coop. So after the camper was running fairly smoothly, he began construction of an A-frame chicken run, followed soon after by setting up a path to the coop with recycled dock sections. He also built garden areas with rock walls, using rocks from the crumbling stone wall around the property. The solar dehydrator was assembled, garden boxes went in, and the kids helped us begin transplanting the seedlings we had started in a makeshift greenhouse back at the old house.

These were days of excitement, hope, and joy. We hosted family and friends around our campfire, explored our land, took lots of pictures, and shared our ongoing story on our blog. It was just the beginning, and we knew it, but there was deep satisfaction knowing it was the beginning of living out our dream.

"Does your converter make a lot of noise?" Our new, camper-dwelling friend texted, around the time we were moving out of our camper.

"Just the fan," Glen responded in his succinct writing style.

"Right now we have two LED lights on and one incandescent and it's making noise. If I turn one more LED on, it stops, but then one more and it starts again."

"If the converter is charging the batteries, it's probably fine. Does the fan run?"

"Yes."

"Then I wouldn't worry about it."

"But it's annoying!"

"Yeah, it is! Welcome to camper living!"

Like a little ant family preparing for winter, those last few months before we moved into the camper were a terribly busy season for us. We knew there would be challenges we couldn't anticipate, especially since we didn't personally know anyone who had done this, but we did our best to research, and plan, and prepare. We read blogs about homesteaders and full time RVers, we watched YouTube videos on purchasing the right equipment and setting it up, and our house became a workshop to prepare all the things we thought we would need to get started.

By the time we arrived, we had a basic system in place to get started with. Glen said he wanted to wait until we were living in the camper to figure out what we actually needed. If we had known others who were doing the same thing, we might not have needed to do it that way, but given how many times we reorganized and updated our system the wait-and-see approach turned out to make the most sense.

Among Glen's many projects, after moving the camper to its more permanent location atop a platform inlaid into the ground, was the issue of water. Although we had set up the awning to collect rainwater in trash barrels, rain was not dependable, and pollen kept clogging up the filters. For the next few years, we depended largely on water we trucked in from Glen's parents. After pumping it into the 20-gallon RV tank, and the water was used, it drained into a small rock and sand pit Glen created where the pipe drained; essentially a mini leach field. There was only a maximum of 50 gallons going through the system each week, so dumping it wasn't a big concern. We began learning how to be super conservative washing dishes and taking showers or baths; turning the water off when it wasn't necessary to have it on. We were still using the RV toilet, but Glen began experimenting with composting it, using peat moss. It was way too watery though, because of the flushing, so we were glad to be done with that mess when Glen changed the toilet into a composting toilet later that year. We didn't need to worry about heat yet, but the last big issue was power. Just to get it set up, Glen bought a single 100-watt solar panel for $330 and two deep cycle batteries, and connected them directly to the RV battery, with a large extension cable going out our bedroom window. If it wasn't for our TV, it probably would have been enough to keep the camper charged. He mounted the solar panel on a deer carrier to make for easy adjustment a few times a day, and soon after he was preparing for a more permanent power set up.

In those first few days, I was busy organizing and reorganizing our belongings, deciding what needed to be in the camper with us, and which things would be better kept accessible in the storage camper. I used every square inch the best I could. The cubby for a microwave became a good spot for big pots and pans. The bench seats hid Lego and games underneath. The one empty spot between the couch and the door now held a book shelf and our low wattage, 24" TV and DVD player. Everything had its own space, and the outdoor living area, with table, fire ring, and Mother's Day plants, took shape as well.

Could we do this? Could we make it work? In the end, we could not have prepared for the challenges that would come, but we stepped out the door and onto the road of adventure with bravery, ready to confront what may come for the joy set before us.

"You can choose courage or comfort, but you cannot have both." ~ Brene Brown

Chapter Two

~Just One Step~

My Nana is one of those people who can take a glance at the grass and immediately spot a four-leaf clover. I have no idea how that works! Every once in a while, I will think of her and plunk myself down in the grass to look for one. From an early age, I would scour the front yard, looking for that lucky clover, but I didn't find my first one until the spring we moved into our camper. I haven't found another one since. I decided to accept this little gift as a sign of our fresh start; that we were on the right path, and everything would work out. That little clover remained taped to the marker board in my bedroom for the longest time, next to important papers and plans, as a secret reminder I would see every time I woke up. This was our chance to hit refresh, and to discover freedom from the culture we found so unsatisfying.

One of the unofficial rules of writing is that an author must never share the details of the story before it is written, lest the drive which motivates them to put pen to paper dissipate. It is also a rule I have been breaking from the beginning, as I have been in the act of sharing our story in progress since before it began.

In 2010, before we had even begun to seriously plan our move, Glen and I started a YouTube channel and a blog. We called it American Family Now. We wanted to give a voice to what we saw as an uprising of American families who were also unhappy living the status quo. The rising new American family standard, representing a group of people who felt passionate standing up for what they believe in and living their lives by it, were also typically libertarian, family focused, God centered, and motivated to "get back to basics."

For the next six or so years, we kept our growing number of followers updated on our experiences, including the highs and lows. Through this platform, people who had been desiring to leap finally did so because of the encouragement they found through our story. I remember the feeling I had the first time we received an email from a follower who said they bought a camper because of us and the words that came out of my mouth. That's about the time I decided to make sure I was completely honest about the trials of this lifestyle; I did not want to feel responsible for people changing their lives!

One follower, in particular, decided to move her little homestead to a friend's farm and live in a camper with her two kids. Call it fate, chance, or a work of God, but this friend of hers was an acquaintance of mine. Neither of us knew we had a mutual connection, but when we finally met in person we quickly became friends and ended up being influential in helping each other to reach our dreams. It is likely that if she hadn't been following me through the blog, none of that would have happened. You might not even be reading this book today if it weren't for her following my blog years ago. It's all connected.

The blog was more difficult to operate from the homestead. We went from unlimited internet to 5GB on one cell phone, with no hotspot ability. Just enough data to check emails each day, and do a bit of research as needed. During the week, Glen would work on video editing offline, I would take photos, write and edit my posts and type them up, and on Friday evenings I would tuck the kids into bed and go down to the local general store, which offered free WiFi to its customers.

It was one of my weekly rituals I looked forward to and which gave me an anchor to hold my week together. The second I sat down in the car, the noise of the children ceased, and on the quiet, but a short ride to the store just down the road, I imagined all I might be able to accomplish with the peace and quiet.

The bell jingled as I entered the old building with creaky wooden floors. I picked out my favorite cream soda, and perhaps a locally made brownie, and stood in line where neighbors were picking up their pizzas or buying gas. When it was my turn I shared a few words with the owner (who also often worked as the cashier), about how things were going with our families. Then I found a quiet

35

corner toward the back of the building where there were picnic tables available to customers and laid out my things: my laptop came out of its bag, my notebook with a to-do list, and of course my purchased snacks. The next hour or two would be spent with no interruptions, aside from an occasionally loud conversation from upfront that sounded entertaining to listen to. When I packed up around 9:30 pm I almost always felt content with the work I had accomplished and was ready for another week of creating videos and posts.

Over time my blogging skills improved; I learned how to schedule posts, embed videos, send group email updates, and so forth. Our internet access improved over time as well; first a little more data and hotspot capabilities, then unlimited data for a year, then a second phone with internet. After a year of these weekly visits, wearing baby Amelia in her wrap near the end, we finally were able to work the blog from home and I stopped going to the store. It was bittersweet, as I enjoyed the conversations with the staff, the routine, and the break from home.

While my internet use was restricted, I enjoyed the disconnection from social media. I didn't have the option of passing spare minutes by scrolling endless feeds. I didn't feel responsible to keep everyone updated on our lives every day. If someone we knew wanted us to know what was going on in their lives they had to call or text us. In September of 2015, we had Facebook again, for the first time in four and a half years. While I do enjoy social media as a form of connection, I also value the time we had without it.

Many people have been following our story since the

beginning. Over time, memories of events became blurry; life happened and notes got mismatched and I hoped I was not forgetting important details. These are two reasons why I hesitated to write again. At this writing, it's been about five years since American Family Now was put to rest, about three years since we moved into our house. I've worried that time has caused me to lose my ability to share the story accurately since even the smallest of details can make the difference between a dry telling of the construction of a house and the rich tapestry that is a family building a home. Some days, I wondered if I should share a certain story on social media or not; I may have wanted the satisfaction of quickly sharing an experience, but I feared whether it would prevent an accurate and passionate retelling in printed form. But that is the definition of a memoir; to share a part of one human's story the way they remember it, to help another human make sense of their own. And so I continue to share ours, through pictures, video, posts, books, and spoken word; to make sense of our story, and hopefully help others to do the same. Someday, it will all come together and make sense.

Those first few weeks flew by. We adapted to the new space, resources, and conservation practices. Every drop of water became precious. Even when we did manage to collect rainwater or water from the dug well for washing, it still had a lot more value than it once had. We saved 550 gallons that summer, which lasted into December when the tank froze. All of our drinking water, and our wash water from January through March, had to be lugged in by 5-

gallon jugs. I joke about how I became the water Nazi. We managed to keep our use down to 50-60 gallons a week by taking twice-weekly baths and showers (the kids taking turns with the bathwater) and rinsing dishes quickly. However, any time the pump turned on, signifying that someone was washing their hands, I would stop what I was doing and wait painfully for them to be done, sometimes losing my patience and just telling them to turn it off already. In comparison, now that we have the ability to store more water, with additional tanks stored in the basement, we use 75-80 gallons of water each week, for showers, dishes, and washing hands and the kids take showers now. We still go to the laundromat to wash our laundry, and even though we now travel to collect spring water, we finally have the ability to filter rainwater with a special filter by AlexaPure.

We did well initially on our little backwoods $500 solar setup, only spending about $20-30 each month on gas to run the generator on cloudy days. In comparison, we now only spend that much on gas during the winter months. Gradually, as finances allowed and the price of solar panels dropped, we expanded and added four more 100-watt panels, an inverter, a converter, and a charge controller, but we have never run anything that uses a lot of power. We still don't have a microwave, a crockpot, or a hairdryer. In the early days, when I wanted to use the blender, I would plug it directly into the generator. That was an interesting sight, and I'm glad I don't need to do that now, though I still need to check the power level before running it from an outlet.

We need to be cautious about what appliances we run at the

same time so we don't shut off the inverter for lack of power. We keep a small meter to monitor the power level and use that to determine, for example, whether the TV can be run without the generator, or if we need to wait till the clouds move from in front of the sun.

Getting used to the appliances was a process; like lighting the gas stove with a BIC lighter for each use, and rotating pans in the oven from the rack to the bottom of the oven, because there was only one small rack. All the regular-sized pans went to the storage camper since there would be no use for them for a long time! Just this year, in 2020, we installed a brand new, full-sized propane oven and range, and an apartment-sized, electric fridge with a compressor to reduce the draw of power. It was a large investment, over $2,000 even with sale prices, but it was high time we let go of the camper appliances!

Organizing the tiny propane fridge, along with the rest of the kitchen space, took time to master after moving into the camper. Learning which items needed to be stored in the fridge, and which ones could be kept on the counter or in a cupboard, instead of putting all fruit, bread, and similar items in the fridge as I once had the ability to do. This was a big change from the giant refrigerator we bought for our old house. Somehow, we still managed to shop for a whole week at a time, but it definitely required new organization skills.

Then there was the trash. Since a trash can would not fit in our small space, we hung grocery bags from the bathroom doorknob to collect garbage. When it was full, it was thrown into a larger bag to take to the dump. In 2013, I built a small dumpster so wildlife would stop ripping holes in trash bags and strewing it all over the yard. The hinges have since broken, but the lid is heavy that it still functions well for us today!

And then the laundry. The hamper was stored, sometimes in the bathtub, sometimes beside our bed, depending on which room I was willing to put up with it in. The smell of wet, dirty laundry while falling asleep is nothing I will ever miss. Once a week, I would pack up the kids and go to the laundromat. I would use money from egg sales to help cover the cost, but eventually, I got so tired of spending what little we had on the dryers that I made a makeshift laundry line at home, between a couple of trees and the old gravity-fed water tower. Even while very pregnant later that year, I would lug all the wet laundry home to hang from the line. Some weeks it would cost as much as $20, but most weeks I could keep it down to $4-6, or less if I sold enough eggs. The backup plan was to wash laundry by hand in the bathtub, but with six people's laundry, I could never bring myself to do it. It would have had its own cost to contend with, such as the extra water we would have had to truck in. One thing I did change, however, was to switch Atlas from cloth diapers to disposable. We much preferred cloth, but the idea of washing them at the laundromat felt inconsiderate.

By the end of May, things had settled down a lot. Spring, and early summer, became all about making new connections in the neighborhood, but it also became a season focused on home and hearth. We got a library card at a new library, we made friends wherever we went, but we were no longer connected online, or in our usual group of friends, and it became a time of focusing inward and on the life that was right in front of us. We had a yard sale Memorial Day weekend and sold the rest of our unneeded belongings, including the infant car seat and all the baby clothes. We were cutting ties with our past to make room for our future.

There may have been a lot on Glen's mind, but the kids thoroughly enjoyed themselves. There was so much to explore and do outside! All the dandelions picked, bamboo forts created, holes dug in the pile of sand by the storage camper, and of course, mud pies made in the play kitchen on our porch. It made us happy to see them settle in, especially after Nemo processed the loss of seeing his friend, "Mr. Epunds," an elderly gentleman who had been friends with our family since before I was born, and whose garage had been next door to our old house. We still saw him every once in a while around town and would say hello.

The days felt slower, though just as busy. We moved the camper to its intended location by the chicken coop on top of a platform made of dock sections, which helped a lot with the leveling! The kids especially appreciated that the amount of water on one side of the tub was now the same as at the other! The view was better, as we could now see the majority of the field, and we could start landscaping around our home. We added extra garden boxes and planters with strawberries and tomatoes and all sorts of goodness. It really was beautiful, and we enjoyed eating produce right from the garden.

In June, I hosted a Pampered Chef party for a friend. We had a great turnout and sat on the deck drinking coffee brewed in a percolator and eating strawberry ice made in a manual food processor; perfect for that warm, sunny day. That was the first event I hosted on our new land, and it felt really good to be welcoming people, in spite of our unconventional living situation.

There was a dark cloud that began looming over us though. Glen had been regularly filling out and submitting job applications, but no one was hiring carpenters. In order to make it worth it, he needed to find a job that would make at least what he did on unemployment. Our budget was already so tight that it was hard to imagine a smaller income, but the only available jobs he could find offered half of his previous income. Once you took out the cost of transportation to get there and added inevitable convenience food expenses, it just wouldn't be worth the time. He did find a couple of odd jobs for people that helped in the short term, but unemployment insurance had a 12 month cutoff. We were now less than six months away. What if he couldn't find work?

Glen took a required class on how to find a job, at the Department of Labor, while I took the kids across the street to the Salvation Army to use change from our change jar to buy summer clothes for Nemo and Daphney. I spent about $14. I used to find such an experience thrilling; now it was humbling. Pinching pennies took on a whole new meaning.

On our blog, I wrote in June: "I like being frugal. I enjoy spending less and finding uses for odd things. Spending more than $10 on a book, or even buying a package of socks costing more than $5 is a splurge for me. Yet despite my interest in tightwad living, I've discovered there is a significant difference between living frugally for enjoyment and living frugally because you couldn't afford shopping even if you wanted to. It still feels good to spend less, to know we can live comfortably without buying everything new whenever we feel like it, but it has required a paradigm shift."

Paradigm shift, indeed. Glen was a high-end finish carpenter. Customers would literally send letters of appreciation to his boss, raving about his work, and request him by name for projects. But there was no work now, and we had lost almost 40% of our income, now having to look at the possibility that we might have to drop it again in order for him to make any money at all. And one of us had to stay with the kids because there was no way we could afford childcare, even if we were open to that. And yet, we went to sleep at night in each other's arms, lulled by the sound of summer rain, trusting in God's goodness, knowing we never had to go without food, clean clothes, warm beds, and a family who loved each other.

In July 2011, the average unemployment rate was 8%, but for carpenters, it was twice that. For every job opening, there were 12 carpenters looking for a job. The housing bubble had burst, and we, along with many others, filed for foreclosure. All I could think about was how grateful I was that we saw it coming. Many others were not so fortunate. Glen began looking into other career options. The Department of Labor was offering a grant to students going for their class A driver's license, because the state was short of drivers. He applied, but only just too late. The program closed because too many students were not following through with applying for jobs afterward. The door closed. We trusted God would take care of us, and He did.

One of the most common questions we got about living in a camper was about our marriage. "You're still together?!" Our relationship was a priority, and we made sure it stayed so. For Independence Day, we took our very first date since Nemo was born five years before. We left them with my parents and spent the night in Old Orchard Beach, walking the beach, listening to the bands play, getting caught in the rain, and eating our fill of ice cream. It was wonderful. We rented a cabin a couple of miles from the ocean, and we walked back and forth between the two. I took the longest hot shower I had had in months. Heaven. But, while we were having a good time, I had a nagging feeling that things were about to change.

My period was late. I took a test when we got home, but it was negative so I soon forgot about it. A week later though, it still hadn't come. I bought some herbs to help me reset my cycle and took one last test to confirm that I wouldn't cause an abortion. Except for this time there were two pink lines. Shit. I couldn't believe what I was seeing. Glen and I sat down on the porch in silence. What were we going to do? "Trust God," he said. "It will all work out." And having no other option, trust we did.

Though I would later come to be saddened by my initial reaction, because I love my baby Amelia beyond words, I had a really hard time connecting to her through the first half of my pregnancy. I kept feeling like I was going to miscarry, until about 20 weeks, probably because I was so worried about providing for four children, and living with them all in a tiny home. Giving birth to and raising a baby in a camper? This was an unexpected plot twist. Just like Frodo, we had definitely been swept off our feet! My midwife was generous and agreed to barter for partial payment and accept the rest after our tax return came, but I was otherwise emotionally detached until well into the fall. I just couldn't think about it yet.

We all had plenty of other things to keep us busy and pass the time. The solar dehydrator was kept full at all times, and we invested a couple of hundred precious dollars into olive oil and vodka so I could make herbal salves and extracts, along with unique tea blends. The goal was to create herbal medicine to sell at parties hosted by family and friends, and after storing a dozen quart-size mason jars in a cubby under the camper for several weeks, I prepared the cute little containers with handwritten labels and carted off my wares in the evenings to sell. It turned out to be worth every penny of the investment. I spent $200 or so and made about $1,700. Little did I know that one day I would become a professional herbalist and consult with people about the use of herbs as my job!

I cut back on my expansion plans for my doula service, Birth a Miracle Services, in preparation for a new child of my own, and instead focused on the growing homestead. We ate most of our garden's produce fresh, but I was able to preserve seven quarts of spaghetti sauce. Oh, that smell! It was so delicious and mouth-watering, and it filled the camper as it simmered away in that giant pot that just barely fit between the stove and the hood. It's one of my favorite parts of harvesting from the garden.

Some days it was so hot, that it would easily reach 100 degrees inside the camper. It just soaked up all the sun, and would easily be 20 degrees hotter inside than out. We might turn on the generator to run the AC (it would be a couple of years before we found a fan with low enough wattage that we felt comfortable running one), but other days we would hop in the car and go for a ride with the windows down and cool off that way. Gotta love the poor man's AC. We took a trip to the ocean, went to a hot air balloon festival, and accepted a last-minute invitation to hike up Streaked Mountain and camp there for the night. That was an adventure! I was almost five months pregnant and carrying one-year-old Atlas on my back, while Glen carried all the luggage for two adults and three children. His backpack was loaded well above his head! Dehydration was an issue for me, but we made it, and we had fun roasting hot dogs around the campfire and even sleeping in our teepee tent on top of blueberry bushes; the softest place we could find.

That August, three months after we filed for foreclosure, we put the house on the market, in a short sale attempt. It looked so sad; sitting there unlived in.

Adventures continued on the homestead. One day, while Papa was away, the first big thunderstorm approached. We listened to the storm around us as the rain came down. Then, for a brief second, silence. There was this, bizarre empty space surrounding us, just for a moment, and then CRACK!! The sound of thunder, extremely loud, occurred at the same moment that I saw a flash of bright light. It was right next to us! I looked out of the window and discovered a large fallen tree under the neighboring overhead power lines where one had not been before. Being in a metal box, lightning was a concern of mine, but there were higher objects around us, so I trusted we would be okay, and we were never struck.

Also in August, we celebrated Daphney's third birthday. She wanted to dress up as a princess, so we hosted a costume party for her friends, and I made her a princess gown with a "hennin," the cone-shaped princess hat, complete with tassel. Nemo wore his bear costume, and I dressed Atlas as a lumberjack. We had a pinata and other games, and everyone had a good time, chilling out in our backyard playing with the kids.

It had been less than four months since we moved, and the real test of our willpower was yet to come, but we were happy. We had decided together, each step of the way, on what was best for our family, and we knew God wasn't just going to drop a provision in our lap without us working for it, but we were optimistic and put one foot in front of the other.

We would need that optimism too because that summer the reality of how things can change very quickly set in. One Friday night, on my way home from the general store, my car died on the side of the road. I called Glen, and he said the fridge had just died. Given how little money we had, this was a discouraging evening, but God did provide for us. The car was fixed with a couple of hundred dollars, and the fridge turned out to simply need to be turned off for a couple of days to reset. Granted, that became an every 6-8 week process, but we were grateful not to need a new one, as it easily costs anywhere from $1,400-2,000 for a propane fridge.

The weather began to turn. Cooler days and even cooler nights, autumn rain, and mud. We began to think more intently about preparing for the winter, and what to do about work. But life continued. We took a camping trip on Labor Day weekend with family, as was the custom. Nemo started PreK at home. Glen stopped his summer work on his brother's house and spent more time working on the homestead. We practiced power conservation as the tilt of the earth changed and we got less daily sunlight; "is there enough sun for that?" My belly grew and I started having regular appointments with my midwife. I started accepting and was almost ready to embrace the fact that we were having another child.

I distinctly remember rushing home from the laundromat one day for a home visit with my midwife, Susi. I wanted everything to be perfect, because I felt so self-conscious about our lifestyle, and I was low on time to make it happen. The wet laundry, which I refused to spend more money on to run through the dryers, needed to be hung up on the makeshift clothesline I concocted. Halfway through, the line snapped and I tried fruitlessly to haul the line back up again, clothes and all, before giving in to the fact that I needed to remove all the clothes and start again. I worried that the stress would raise my blood pressure and set a bad impression. At the end of the day, the laundry was hung up and the visit had gone well.

Clothes drying weather became rare though. We had so much rain that autumn that everything was always wet. There was literally a river of water running under the camper. Mold was a constant battle because everything was so damp and humid. I packed all the kids' clothes into plastic tubs so they weren't collecting the moisture off the back wall of their cabinet, and we packed up Nemo's bike, Daphney's scooter, Atlas' riding tractor, and started taking regular trips to a nearby track to escape the mud. That became a regular outing until the snow stopped melting and winter settled in.

Among the choices we laid out on the table to ensure housing through the winter included the possibility of staying put, moving back into our house in foreclosure until they locked us out, finding a cheap apartment, or moving in with family. We priced out each option, compared the pros and cons. We had talked to everyone as if we were staying, but we weren't so stubborn that we would stay if it didn't make any sense. After weighing all our options though, we decided to stick with the original plan, with a backup plan to pack essentials and move in with family for the winter if necessary, and it was also crucial that we build a closed in porch against the camper to offer it shelter and provide extra living space.

This he did begin to build, using material he bartered for from his brother, but when he ran out of materials and money, we thought we would have to move. At just the right time, an early Christmas gift arrived, and the porch was able to be closed in! Each piece was carefully and resourcefully designed. The windows came off the porch of our old house, and we planned to reuse the plywood, timbers, and hopefully roofing on our new house.

A Nor'Easter dropped 15" of snow on Halloween Eve, putting

a damper on construction. Though there was a lot of shoveling to do, we were grateful not to be among the 100,000+ Mainers without power. We enjoyed French toast for breakfast, corned beef for supper, and played games with the kids all day. The sunlight at the end of the day reflected off the snow and created the most beautiful scenery. We pulled snow gear from the storage camper for the kids and they were delighted to play outside.

When work resumed on the porch, it was like someone had turned the heat back on: the snow melted, and Atlas was comfortably playing on the porch floor in his diaper while Glen constructed the rest of the framing around him. The porch extended the length of the camper with plywood floor and walls, and metal roofing. There were three walls, with the front of the camper making up the fourth side, and we stuffed spare insulation around the edges to stop snow and wind from blowing in around the camper. We weren't able to insulate it, but the big picture window on the front side let in lots of sunlight and kept it warm. A big plywood door with a simple wooden lock was built on the end, and closest to the driveway.

One of my favorite things was just how much our days were filled with joy. In October that year, I wrote, "If a family is going to rise above hard times they need to be willing to let go of their problems and cling to each other... and if we are going to enjoy each other, and our life, then we can't let these temporary problems hold us back." And hold us back, they did not.

In no particular order, that fall we went apple picking, for a ride on the Cog Railway with family (the perfect outing for our young train enthusiast), raked and jumped in piles of leaves with friends and turned it into a fun homeschool lesson, celebrated Nemo's fifth birthday at a nearby park with a crowd of family around us, and the day before his birthday, Nemo accepted Jesus Christ as his savior. Our hearts were full.

Being young, the kids had a limited understanding of why we lived differently, but they made the most of it. By shopping carefully and doing lots of baking, we brought our grocery bill down to $75 a week. The kids all loved that I was baking frequently; they would gather around the table to beg for a bite of dough, a lump to play with, or just swipe their fingers across the table to lick. Their little eyes sparkled, and I knew everything would be okay.

As the days cooled, we spent more time inside. The kids were still small enough that we had spaces to retreat to when we needed time alone. One might be curled up on the couch, another on my bed, someone at the table, and of course their own beds were always open for quiet (or loud!) play. I had my Friday nights at the store, and somehow we just learned to enjoy being closer physically more of the time, while also giving each other space. Quiet, imaginary play toys, books, art projects, and other common children's toys found their places throughout the camper. One of my own favorite pastimes was crocheting Christmas gifts. Many evenings were spent crocheting in front of the TV!

While we definitely did not appreciate the added heating costs, we all enjoyed the coziness of the kerosene heater, warm sweaters, the beauty of fall, and the autumn urge to create, design, and imagine; moving from the physical work of summer to the mental work of winter.

Sometimes I wonder if the idealistic view of living off-grid or in a tiny home clouds the vision of the dreamer. The way I hear people talk about it, it's as if the problems of this world simply disappear when you decide to live an unusual lifestyle. Maybe, to some degree, I hoped the same would happen to us. Yet normal life issues found us nonetheless, in our little corner of the world, in the middle of nowhere. Our days were filled with normal parenting struggles: nap times, potty training, tantrums, and yes, homeschooling. We did our best to separate the anxiety of our financial struggles from the struggles of normal life.

One of the lowest moments for me was when we brought our little Camry to the mechanic to get an inspection sticker (the same one we had just sacrificed a few hundred dollars for) and were told the frame was so rusted out that it wasn't worth a new sticker. In Maine, a rusted frame equals the death of a car. All the salt used to keep our roads from being too slick in the long winter months is bad for vehicles, and eventually, they give in to the repeated attacks, and generally, by then, the frame is not worth replacing, because of the age of the vehicle. But that car had been part of our plan; we were going to sell it and use the money to buy a vehicle that could fit our whole family after the baby came. Now we didn't have a car, and no money to buy a new one. I cried. We were trying so hard to do all the right things, for what purpose?

Just when it seemed like we were running out of options, and less than a month before the unemployment insurance would run out, Glen got a call back about one of his many job applications. He was hired as a project manager and later promoted to plant supervisor, of the last start-to-finish wood product manufacturing plant in all of New England. It paid a bit less money than his old job, and with another child, we weren't able to take on the mortgage again, but it was only 13 miles from home, there was room to grow, and it had sentimental value as well: Glen's dad used to work there, in a similar position.

We were so grateful, but also in a bit of shock. Glen had been home for almost a year, for more than half of young Atlas' life, and even when he had an odd job to do, he was still accessible. Now, with just a few days' notice, he was gone for ten hours a day, just like that.

In a strange way, it felt like we lost him. A few days after Thanksgiving, I wrote, "The kids were more fussy, unable to explain their malcontent. The water tank ran low and I didn't know how to fill it. The battery died and I couldn't start the generator. Papa came home to find me cooking by the light of a lantern. And only one blessed hour between his arrival home and the kids' bedtime." It wasn't an odd job; this would be happening again. And again. And again. The bittersweet reality sunk in. Glen began teaching me how to take over the chores he had been doing; how to fill the water tank, switch the propane tanks, reset the power, and so on. That generator would always be a pain to start, but I remember the day I purchased and replaced the inverter for the first time; I was quite proud of myself! During one snowstorm that winter, very heavy with child, I struggled to start the generator, which was not dependable. I hauled on that cord so many times, and of course, it was always in a blizzard that it would refuse to start.

Glen may have been hired, but those first few weeks were really difficult. Because of the new pay cycle and the way unemployment weans you off payments, we went from less than $300 a week to no money for three weeks. We had to borrow money for groceries that last week. As hard as it was to ask for help, I figured we had done pretty well to get this far and only need to borrow a vehicle for a while and money for a week's worth of groceries. We were fortunate. Two friends we knew were laid off. The recession was far from over. We saved as much of Glen's new paychecks as we could.

People began asking us why we were staying in the camper when Glen now had a job. It was like, somehow, they thought everything would go back to normal. After going through all that though, even if we made different arrangements, normal would forever look different. Unemployment changes you. Sometimes these comments came from well-meaning people, some were in the form of nasty comments left on our YouTube channel, but the majority of people were actually quite understanding.

We weren't the only ones who realized the futility of grasping at straws to make the old system work. And even among those who were able to make it work understood and encouraged us for taking the road to freedom. We still wanted to build our own house, debt-free, off-grid, self-sustainable, so no one could take it from us. We hadn't really been able to wrap our heads around how to make this happen, but with a new job, it became safe to dream again. Maybe someday it would happen after all.

The sound of the all familiar truck engine driving into the yard produced the new expected response. Three young children jumped up from wherever they were, and whatever they were doing and ran to the door. They squealed with delight as the door opened and his face shined with pleasure at the love being poured out on him. Those little voices yelling, "Hi Papa!" and spewing out details of all the things they had done that day, because they couldn't wait to tell him. This became the evening transition to home life. Welcome home, Papa.

The second snowstorm came in November. This time the air had cooled down enough that we knew the snow would stick around for a while. It might even be here to stay for the winter. It was also the first storm Glen had to drive to work in from our new home. Though his boss was gracious about the possibility of being late due to the storm, Glen was able to beat the worst of the storm there and arrived before a lot of the snow fell. The ride home was not as kind. Our road hadn't been plowed all day, and there was a nice layer of ice under the snow. After making it down the steep section of our road, he got the truck stuck in the middle of the street, and even after getting it to the end of our driveway, he was understandably anxious and frustrated. We still didn't have a way to clear snow from the driveway, we didn't have a vehicle that could get up and down our hilly yard easily, and we didn't have a plan for getting water to the camper through the winter. On the day of that same storm, the generator died again, and Glen was ready to move. "This isn't going to work!" he yelled on the phone by the road. But after venting his frustration, he remembered how hard he had worked to get us to this point, and realized he didn't want to quit yet. He wasn't ready to throw in the towel, no matter how bleak things looked at the moment.

My grandfather had a second snowblower that he wasn't using, so we arranged a rent-to-own deal with him, which enabled Glen to keep our driveway clear enough for walking at least, and we purchased a rugged sled to haul tanks of water, groceries, and bags of laundry up and down the icy driveway. Evening walks home after visiting with family were the best. I carried Atlas in a backpack and Papa pulled the sled with jugs of water from his parents' spigot and we all walked up the hill in the dark, watching the stars in between our steps to make sure we didn't slip. It was so peaceful. And every day we got a little better prepared for the winter, and more adjusted to the new season's rhythms.

The days zoomed by and we spent our time taking care of children, chickens, work, and getting ready for winter, but even as we had plenty of things to keep us busy, the tension began rising between Glen and me. He would come home from work and I would unload my day on him, and he would do the same to me, but for some reason, it never seemed to bring the release that these conversations used to have. About midway through December, we finally took an available chance and stayed up late into the night to talk about what was happening.

At the root of the tension, it turned out, was grief. We had been mourning the loss of the 11 months we had just spent together almost nonstop. Add that to the exhaustion we both felt about doing the hard work of our jobs and living a new and difficult life, and we were just feeling really confused about how to express ourselves to each other, without adding overwhelm and frustration to the other person's plate. As is often the case, just talking about it took away the power of the negativity. The elephant in the room was finally spoken about, and its power was crippled. Now that we understood each other more clearly, even on hard days we had an unspoken understanding and more grace for each other. The hardships even felt easier to handle knowing the other just understood.

The remainder of the autumn, which is really more like winter in Maine, was spent making plans for our baby's birth, sorting through the "giant closet" (otherwise known as the storage camper) for winter clothes, rearranging the kids' bedroom to make room for a baby in the 4th bunk, and preparing for Christmas.

While Glen was at work building runner sleds in what had come to feel to him like Santa's workshop, I played Christmas music at home and got creative with decorating for Christmas. I hung the stockings from the curtain rod over the couch, we put a Christmas tree on the porch, and hung LED Christmas lights around the ceiling with tacks, powered by the inverter. It was unconventional, but it felt like Christmas.

The kerosene heater, vented by keeping the windows and

vents cracked throughout the camper, kept us plenty warm and cozy, and I continued finishing up the homemade gifts I had been making that autumn; scarves, ornaments, and similar items. We had only recently started getting a paycheck, but that little boost came at just the perfect time. Though we have a lot of family, we spent less than $300 altogether on Christmas, and the kids still had many of the things they wanted. We enjoyed the giving and receiving. After the kids went to bed on Christmas eve, we put tiny, decorated trees on the table and put all of the gifts underneath. It was beautiful! I was so grateful that after everything, we were able to give our kids gifts and make it special.

In the morning, we played Christmas music and opened all the presents. The kids and I bought Glen a lunch box and long johns. He and the kids bought me slippers and insulated mittens. The slippers are long gone now, but I still wear the mittens each year! We joked about this being our first and hopefully last Christmas in the camper, Glen worked on the frozen pipes, and then we went to his parents' house for dinner. Even though the pipes were frozen, and other issues existed, Christmas was truly a hopeful time, we laughed with the kids, and we believed that no matter what happened, we would be okay.

The two weeks around Christmas that year were a flurry of activity, and not just because of the holidays. I also attended a birth, we went to the laundromat for the first time in almost two weeks and a dryer someone was using started smoking, and in the same week that the toilet needed replacing because the sewer tank froze, we all started coming down with the stomach bug.

I was the first one to get sick, at six months pregnant. Glen was hurrying as fast as he could to replace the RV toilet with a compost toilet, which was a fancy way of saying a five-gallon pail hidden by a wooden box with a toilet seat. I threw up a couple of times in a bucket on the porch, but I was so grateful when I could use the bathroom and close the door! I had been concerned about what it would be like to get sick in the camper, but it turns out that as long as you have a place you feel comfortable resting and a toilet or bucket to throw up in you, you're good!

Changing over the toilet wasn't quite that simple for Glen. If he could go back, he would have taken care of it before the sewer tank froze. It made the job loathsome. I'm sure your mind can fill in the blanks. Once the toilet was out and the pipe area was clear, he covered over the exposed pipe hole with plywood. He built a wooden box over the plywood piece, tall enough to cover a five-gallon pail, put a hole in the top to allow maneuvering of the pail in and out of the bathroom, and attached a toilet seat to the box in such a way that by lifting the seat, you could pull the pail out to empty it. We had a couple of dumpsites for the waste to go. It was a fairly straightforward process, but in summer he tended to avoid emptying it right before folks came over, because the breeze would carry the smell of fresh waste matter quite far! The toilet worked well though and served us for the remaining time we spent in the camper. A similar design still works for us today and will continue to until the permanent compost toilet is finished.

The days sped by. I wrote in my blog that our days were rarely quiet, usually busy, but that they had a rhythm that I had come to appreciate. In the morning, Glen would go off to work. When the kids woke up we would have breakfast, read the Bible, do a half hour of schoolwork (Nemo was in PreK and Daphney in preschool), followed by some straightening up and outdoor play while Atlas napped. After lunch, we would often read together or do crafts. Supper was on the table at about 5 pm, shortly after Glen had returned home, the kids were in bed at 6:30, and then Glen and I worked on our own projects and visited until we went to bed.

Until baby Amelia arrived, my cleaning practices had a predictable routine to them, when I stopped to think about it. Mondays were a general cleaning day, picking up the mess from the weekend. That took about an extra hour. Tuesday was laundry day: packing up the kids with books to read and hauling them and the laundry down the hill in the snow, driving to the laundromat, washing, and drying, driving back home, hauling the laundry back up the hill, folding it all, and putting it away. Thursdays I cleaned the bathroom, and Fridays I cleaned the porch the best I could with its clutter. Every day I swept and washed dishes. I didn't keep the camper spotless by a long shot, but it was comfortable, healthy, and safe, and we made room and time for our hobbies and things we enjoyed doing together.

We all had plenty of things to entertain us too. I clearly remember helping Nemo set up his entire Thomas the Train set, which extended from one end of the camper to the other and trying to keep Daphney and Atlas otherwise preoccupied so that poor track would be left alone! Daphney had her dollhouses we would set up on the table, everyone had Lego, and Atlas was always happy just to be included.

Nemo was particularly concerned about keeping his siblings out of his stuff, so we purchased totes to put in each of their beds so that special toys they didn't want to share could be moved from accessible, shared space under the beds to their own bunks. He was relieved, I think both that we responded to his concern, and that it was taken care of.

Glen continued to tweak his music hobby, trading in music equipment for more compact and versatile pieces. Eventually, he would have his travel sized electric guitar and all the processors and recorders and other tools for music that I don't understand would all be on his iPad. Learning how to do what we wanted in a smaller space was a challenge, but one that thrived on our creative skills.

To make even more space, especially as nesting became a more prominent activity in our lives, Glen removed one of the RV benches from the dining area and replaced it with a stool and our clip-on highchair. Taking out that huge bench, though it removed some storage space, felt so freeing. It cleaned up almost five square feet, which felt so huge in our 200 square foot home! It also turned out to play a helpful role in Amelia's birth, as you'll soon see.

We had a lot to be thankful for that winter. We were given food pantry donations, a borrowed car, bartering for our midwife's services, the temperature stayed almost consistently at 20-30 degrees, and we didn't have a lot of snow after the early Nor'Easters. The chickens lived well on snow and food scraps, and we were getting five eggs a day from the ten birds. We had money to buy gender-neutral clothes for our coming baby, and our confidence in living off-grid was growing. It actually occurred to me, deep into the winter, that I was no longer afraid of strangers or wild animals, appearing suddenly while I was out there alone in the woods with my nearly four babies. I was becoming more secure in my environment, and we were all becoming more accustomed to our new life.

Though we did take precautions with venting the kerosene heater, horror stories about what happens to people who aren't careful did not lose their impact on me. We frequently cleaned the wick, and let the heater burn out as often as we could to allow for better wicking of the fuel, but it inevitably smelled strong of kerosene, and on days when windows had to remain closed and the wick was particularly dirty, the camper stunk so bad that I was concerned about the quality of the air we were breathing. Every now and then I would find a reason to take the kids into town so we could breathe some fresh air, and it was not unusual for me to get up during the night to check on the kids for the first few weeks into each winter. Logically, I know this was a fear-based reaction, but it was nonetheless something I had to contend with.

The winter waned and Amelia's birth was nearly upon us. We hosted friends and their kids for dinner, putting people and food wherever we could find room. It helped that the kids were all still small! Spaghetti dinners were the best. The kids also enjoyed playing outside in the snow. The gently sloping hill was just perfect for small children to go sliding without getting hurt. After one particular snowstorm, the snow was too sticky for them to really get their own path going, so eight-month pregnant mama helped them start the first course! Also in those last weeks of winter, we replaced our two batteries for the solar system, bought six chicks who lived in a plastic tote with no lid that took over the space our Christmas tree had taken, and we were finally able to purchase a vehicle with our tax return: a Durango with a third row seat. For a few weeks, we were able to drive up and down the hill with its four wheel drive, which was such a huge blessing! Things were looking up.

About a week before Amelia was born, we had to leave the Durango at the bottom of the hill by the road, because the weather had warmed up so much that the snow was melting faster than the ground could absorb it. This turned out to be a thing on our property. Needing something to do to pass the time, I raked the ruts into the ground that week as best I could. Right around my due date we also took a trip to the library and to walk around the tennis court (one of few dry places I could find). I needed so much to take my mind off the changes taking place in my body; I was so anxious to meet little Amelia.

I woke up Thursday morning, March 22nd. Glen had gone to work and the kids were calling for breakfast. Something felt different. I couldn't explain it. The contractions I had been having for weeks continued as before, but somehow I knew it was time. I didn't want to get too hopeful though, so I waited until about 9:30 am to text my mom and Glen. I told them not to come, but to know they should be on alert. My mom came anyway. She needed to be my mom. She took care of the kids and sat with me, putting up with my ramblings as I processed what was happening. At some point, she suggested that I call the midwife, so I called and told her my contractions were changing, but not to come yet. She had a prenatal to give and then she'd check in with me.

The weather was absolutely beautiful. It was sunny and a record breaking 80 degrees. The kids were playing in mud puddles and I baked a birthday cake; a tradition I started for each of my babies. The contractions came every few minutes, but I could still carefully talk through most of them. Glen came home at about 4 pm and picked up the kids to bring them to his parents. We walked down the hill to meet him, and I'm not sure if it was the walking or the letting go of my kids, but as soon as I got back to the camper the contractions finally said, "we're not fooling around anymore," and just like that I was in active labor. The midwives were on their way, Glen was back by 5 pm, and the primary midwife soon after.

My water broke while I was lying in bed and I waddled as quickly as I could to the bathroom. I had felt it pop, but managed to get there before it made a mess! The next couple of hours, donning my Depends, went by in a blur. I walked the field, leaning on Glen during contractions. I sat in a chair on the porch, skimming through Facebook between contractions. I ate spinach soup my mom had lovingly made for me. Around 7 pm, I started coaching myself through contractions and said I wanted to go back inside. I told them that the other midwife, who had been sitting in her car in the driveway to avoid being in the way, should come in.

Sitting on the couch, with my midwife rubbing my shoulders, I breathed and moaned and got really focused. I remember all of a sudden feeling a plunk of the baby's head into my pelvis. I looked at the clock in front of me. 7:25 pm. I said I was going to be pushing soon, so it was suggested that I try to go pee. I stood up to go to the bathroom, and no sooner had I stood up, but I suddenly had a massive desire to push. I wasn't going anywhere! I was pushing right here, standing by the couch and leaning over the dining room table in my tiny home, surrounded by my mom, my husband, and my two midwives, one of whom was thankfully by my head giving me words of affirmation because I was totally freaking out. I may have had three babies already, but it never made this part easier. "Oh my God!" I screamed, which is like the f-bomb for me. And out came her head. The primary midwife, Glen, and my mom had worked quickly to pull off my pajama pants and rip off the Depends, just in time for her head to finish crowning and pop out. As I pushed out her body into Glen's and the midwife's hands, I looked down between my legs and all I saw was little girl parts! They handed her up to me and helped me to sit back down on the couch, wrapping blankets around us both. I was so out of breathe. I found out later, she was born at 7:28 pm. Three minutes after I said I needed to push soon. No wonder I was out of breath!

Three hours later, Glen, Amelia (all 9lbs 14oz of her), and I had settled into bed and the midwives and my mom had left. The sound of some art show on PBS played in the background. The kids would be home in the morning, Glen would be here for a few days, and we had help lined up for a couple of weeks. All was right in the world.

And on a high, we certainly were! We had just given birth to our fourth child, and we had nearly made it a year in our camper, all the way through the winter. We would need that energy to keep us hopeful because ten days later, things took a not entirely unexpected, but a sharp change in direction.

I was nursing Amelia on the couch and the kids were playing around me when I heard a voice from outside. "Hello?" I didn't recognize it, and given that we had been obsessed with no one finding out where we lived, this unfamiliar voice made me feel uncomfortable. Amelia was made to stop nursing, and I left her crying with Nemo, while I went outside to investigate.

The older gentlemen introduced himself as the code enforcement officer. My heart sunk to my stomach. "I didn't know anyone was up here!" He said. "We got a call that someone was up here in a camper and I just came to find out what's going on. How long have you been here?" He could clearly see we had been here through the winter. No one would be able to get a camper set up there now during mud season anyway. I decided to play dumb. "I don't really know!" I said with a smile. "Six months?" He asked. "Maybe, I'm not sure. I would have to ask my husband." He must have thought that I was either simpleminded or knew I wasn't telling the truth. "Okay, well, here's my business card. Have him give me a call." Phew! He was gone. Now we could regroup and figure out what our approach was going to be. But first, Amelia needed to finish her second breakfast.

Given how careful we had been; no mailbox, no driving in when people were behind us, no telling people other than family and friends where we lived, and so on, we couldn't think how the code enforcement had figure it out. And then suddenly the dots connected. Our midwife had filed Amelia's birth certificate... with the town office. I could only imagine the conversation. "Number 20? I don't have anyone listed at that location on that road. Are you sure you have the address correct?" And badda bing badda boom: code enforcement to the investigation!

Glen and I were a bundle of nerves about the whole thing. We had no idea what the rules were. We had taken the "act first, apologize later" approach, and it seemed the time had come to apologize. We didn't know how forgiving this man would be, however or if we would have to pack up and start again somewhere else.

Thankfully, the CEO offered us both understanding and grace. After Glen shared our story and laid it out on the table, he responded by saying that he respected that we were trying to get back on our feet and that he knew others who had lived similarly. He told us what we needed to do to meet minimum requirements, and was very patient about the whole thing. We would need a permit for the porch we had already built, along with a permit and plan for a gray water leach field and an outhouse to use as a dumpsite for our compost toilet. Once we had those taken care of, and a plan drawn up to get a building permit and a plumbing permit for a house, we could live in our camper indefinitely as long as we were doing some work consistently on the house.

The plans for the leach field and outhouse we hired out for, as required, soon after. Thankfully, Glen had been picking up some extra hours, so we were able to pay for the permits and the materials to build the outhouse and leach field. Though it came as a surprise, it was good to have answers and a concrete direction for our homestead project for the summer. We had received permission to be here and could relax a bit. We could get a mailbox in and meet more of the neighbors. We could start planning for our house, for our future.

Trying to keep the town happy was a continuous thought process going on in the back of our minds, but the kids played on, blissfully unaware of the potential seriousness of our situation. And that was exactly how we wanted it to be for them. Every day, I took walks around the field with Amelia strapped to me in a baby wrap. I attempted to make science lessons out of the spring blossoms for the kids, but they were just too excited to play to pay attention.

Nemo started climbing trees in earnest that spring. One afternoon, as I was doing my rounds of the field, I looked over just in time to see him fall about five feet. All I could think was that he had landed on sharp branches or rocks, but as I started running over, he quickly stood up, proclaiming his well being. "I'm okay!" He was our little daredevil. Within a few years, he would be climbing to the very top of that same tree, probably 30 feet high.

The chickens also made fun playmates for the kids. We had two roosters, a handful of hens, and two ducks. Nemo and Daphney would help us find the hidden eggs and take turns throwing the ones of unknown age on the ground to watch them splatter. Our feathered friends always hung out wherever we were, so our doorstep was generally covered with chickens. If the kids ate outside, they had to be careful to avoid sharing their food, as the hens would come right up to them and eat off their plates. One day, a friend came to visit, who shares my blonde hair color. Her arrival was marked by her cries for help, and I looked out the window to see hens chasing her for the food scraps they assumed she was carrying!

Nemo, Daphney, and Atlas enjoyed their growing freedom outdoors, and while Amelia napped, I dug into the cleaning project that was the porch. It had become a storage area for all things we didn't have room for in the camper; water barrels, toys, jackets and boots, recycling, and so much more. I much prefer to focus on a job till it is done, but with a one month old baby, I had to work with what I had, so one hour at a time over the course of a few days, I organized, shuffled, packed, and trashed until the porch was opened and transformed into a play area with a table and chairs. Glen built shelves for games and books, and very slowly, we added living space to our home until it was double in size. A whole 400 square feet; the size of many living rooms.

Glen caught the remodeling bug and built a new table for the dining area. This one folded up so we could easily move it out of the way when desired, but it also remained unattached to the floor, so we could push it against the wall under the big window, to create a little extra floor space when we needed it. Once the benches were built into the L shaped wall, and stools were added, we had plenty of room for our family, or for extra children to sit when we had guests.

Sunday, May 6th, 2012 was a beautiful sunny day, and our hearts were as bright and full as the sun, as we all hopped in the car to go to Glen's parents' for dinner. We pushed aside our ongoing concerns about what the next steps were to create our homestead, set down our dreams about the two of us working from home, brushed aside growing worries about overreaching government possibly provoking a move out of state, and we sat there in the car and smiled. We did it. We had lived an entire year off grid in a camper, in the middle of Nowhere Maine, with four kids.

Looking back on this year, we sometimes wonder what it would have been like, or how it would have turned out, if we had done things differently, or if we even COULD have done things differently. When people ask us this question; what we would have done differently to make our experience easier or more successful in the early days, Glen and I agree that we probably would not have moved out of our house as soon as we stopped making mortgage payments. The house was not officially foreclosed on for at least another year, and even though a winter of heating bills would have been difficult for us to pull off, we could have had several more months at the least to help us transition to the new land.

The second thing Glen thinks that would have made our new life easier would have been using the seven grand we spent on a camper to build an equivalent-sized cabin and outfit it with appliances. It may not have saved us any money, but we would have been able to customize it how we wished, and avoid some of the complications that unfortunately come with camper living, like the single pane windows that make condensation and mold growth inevitable, or thin walls for mice to easily chew their way in.

People would write to us through our blog and tell us they wanted to do the same thing, or that they were in a financial crisis as well and that our path looked like the best one for them to follow. The truth is, there is no best path, and no two paths will look the same. We had a goal to use our crisis as an opportunity to start fresh. We wanted a home no one else had a claim to, and we wanted to prepare for hardship in general so that no matter what happened, we would be okay. But our path, if others attempted to follow, would be unique to them. It can only happen that way, both in the general term and how we live out the path, day by day. How we lived and continue to live may be completely different for us than for others, and that's okay. It's our story, and no matter how many times we look back and second guess, it unfolded exactly how it needed to, for us to get to where we are today. As the saying goes, there comes a point, where you have to stop living someone else's story and write your own. This year in a camper was simply the first chapter in our own story. We had no way of knowing at the time if it would work out, but as Rumi so famously said, "maybe seeing if it does will be the best adventure ever."

Chapter Three

~A New Path to Beat~

The first year was in the books. Now that we knew we could do it, that we could actually make it out here and find our way, it was time to start looking ahead. We needed a plan, something more concrete than simple wishes to build an off-grid house. The town was waiting on us for a building plan, our family was anticipating a concrete plan of action, and we also needed something more sure to trust in.

No matter what kind of plan we created, we knew that there was a distinct possibility it would not turn out the way we wanted it to. This wasn't like sitting down with a bank and a general contractor and just making it happen. We knew that circumstances were likely to change as we went along, and so any plan we created would be more like a sketch, an outline that would be filled in as it happened in real life. And that was okay, as long as we kept our eyes on the prize and continued moving forward toward the ultimate goal.

After the code enforcement officer paid his first visit at the end of March 2012, we purchased a building permit for the porch over our camper, and one for the septic system. Over the summer, Glen built the outhouse along the treeline and painted the decorative door barn red. Between him and my uncle, the gray water leach field was constructed in the far corner of the field, and we began our long battle to keep the camper's gray water draining into the system built for our future house. Until the house was permanently connected, it consisted of temporary pipes there were connected above ground, from the camper to the leach field (which meant they could only be used in the summer), had to be disconnected to mow the lawn, and they would often pop apart on their own.

Many evenings would find Glen at our little dining room table, with graph paper and ruler in hand, trying to design the most conservative home that would give us ample room with the least amount of special order materials. As excited as we were to get a plan into the hands of our code enforcement officer in exchange for a permit and permission to continue living in the camper, that plan would change a few more times before it would become the final plan that we actually enacted. Thankfully, due to Glen's building experience, there was very little he needed to change for town approval. The first plan, which never had the chance to be sketched out, was to build a house on posts, instead of a concrete foundation. Next, it was a saltbox-style house, which was drawn up but never submitted, and finally, a two-story home with a single-pitch roof so that we could collect all the rainwater on one side and save money on roof rafters. Once our final plan was submitted, two things were required to be adjusted. One was the design of the staircase to the second floor, and the other was the height of the ceilings to accommodate the large windows we had chosen to let in extra light.

By late October 2012, the leach field was complete, and my uncle had dug a few holes to test sites for the future house foundation with his tractor, in between giving rides to the kids. Atlas spent many hours standing along the path of his tractor, watching him move dirt. We wanted to see how far down the ledge was at different locations on the property, to help us determine the most suitable place for the house. After we realized that the entire cleared area of land was covered in ledge, not more than three feet under the topsoil at any given point, we decided to avoid spending money on blasting and just build right on top of the ledge. We broke ground one unceremonious day in November, and my uncle came back in the spring to finish digging out the area down to the ledge. We were ready.

Moving forward on the development project was not as straightforward when it came to family. And for that story, I need to back up a little bit. The 20 acre plot we are sitting on had been given to Glen's mother from a cousin of her own mother's in 2006, the year our firstborn child, Nemo was born. To keep things right between the rest of the family, she and Glen's dad decided to pay for the land, and immediately turned around and deeded five-acre plots to Glen and his brother. After the town approved this, they changed their minds and requested that the three plots be melded together again for a few years, so we all agreed to play nice, and the rights to the land were returned to Glen's parents the same year, despite how silly the whole thing seemed. The last thing we all wanted, was to be on the bad side of the town where some of us might be building in the future.

Glen was laid off and began his 11-month unemployment in December 2010, and knowing we would eventually be given a small plot of the property, we decided to move to the land sooner than we had originally talked about doing. Even though enough time had passed that they could have signed over our plot around the time that we moved, we encouraged Glen's parents to keep the land in their name, so that if our mortgage company decided to seize our assets when we foreclosed on the house, they wouldn't be able to take our new home.

Glen's parents continued to maintain the property; mowing the field every few weeks and clearing a spot under the trees for their own camper. They had plans drawn up for their own house, and dreamed of having a beautiful home on the same land as one of their sons. Sharing property, especially when the piece our home was established on was not legally ours, was an awkward struggle for a while. As Glen's dad worked to make his own dreams happen and sought to establish his place on the land and in a landlord relationship with his son, it temporarily put a damper on things. Frequent arguments occurred between the two of them, over how we were developing the plot we parked ourselves on (not the one we were originally deeded), or what they wanted to do with the land. I remember one conversation that ended badly over the legitimacy of a potential spring on the land. It became a sensitive area of topic, that didn't let up until well into the second year after the town accepted our building plans, which thankfully relieved some of his dad's concerns. Yet, he would still occasionally wield the power of his ownership of the land, which led me to question for a while if this move was the best for us. The last thing I wanted was for our choices to cause conflict in sacred family relationships. As time passed and emotions calmed, we put up with the odd landlord joke and continued as planned. Eventually, in an unexpected turn of events, his dad began bringing their friends up to see his son's homestead. He was accepting and proud in his own way, and we felt new confidence moving forward with our house plans.

As usual, I continued writing selectively about our ongoing experiences on our blog; about three to four posts a week. We were known to the world as Mama, Papa, Buddy, Girlie, Pal, and Chickie. In April, I also started collecting stories from my journal and the blog that occurred over the course of our first year, to write a book called A Year In a Camper. With baby Amelia nursing in the crook of my left arm, I would write with the opposite hand, often after the other three kids had gone to bed and before I was too tired to think. Sitting at the table on the porch while Glen worked on his own project or played guitar, I would write. And though it was a roughly written book, I finished typing it on the laptop I purchased in October with the money I earned as a doula and published it on December 3, 2012. The initial profits were saved for the construction of our new home.

Strangers who heard our story, and people I knew well, would tell me how patient I was and express awe that I would be able to live in the camper for that long with all my kids, home all day. I would smile back and say things like, "You adapt to the space you have," "we take it one day at a time," or "we're keeping our eyes on the goal." Those things were all true, but what I didn't fully understand myself at the time, was that I had begun to struggle with feelings of overwhelm and depression. I took it one day at a time because I had to. If I looked up I was afraid I would lose faith entirely. I would go weeks without seeing people other than Glen's parents, the postman, and the librarian, and I even made friends with the tenant who lived next to the laundromat. I was desperate for community, and I couldn't go anywhere because we didn't have much money to spare for gas. Glen even did the grocery shopping on his way home from work to save gas; all the fewer faces for me to see.

The kids were difficult; especially my second oldest, Daphney. I once took a spirited child test for the kids. On a scale of 0 being easy and 30 being a mother killer, Nemo hit a high of 21, and Daphney, 24. They have grown easier over the years, but 2009-2014 were extremely difficult, parenting wise. Out of respect for them, I won't share specific details, but let's just say, being stuck in 200 square feet with all four of them was the most trying way I have ever spent the long winter months of New England, though I have lived here my entire life.

I struggled to understand my identity, my role, the lack of community, and trying to love my kids while emotionally holding them at arm's length so I wouldn't lose myself. I would get angry and yell, I would bury myself in projects, I would try to look for the positive and be grateful every day. Glen, having his own struggles, couldn't understand mine, and would simply make jokes about me getting a job that would replace his income so we could switch roles and I could get out of the camper. Thankfully by 2014, I was feeling those hard days beginning to come to an end, but as I will explain later, a whole new emotional battle would present itself then.

Would living in a bigger home and not having an interruption to our income have made it easier to cope with my difficult children? Quite possibly, but God's grace saw me through. That was the real answer to the comments people made about my choices. God's love and grace are why I stayed and turned out okay. Reading and learning about spirited children helped me to gain peace about parenting small, active children. From such books, I came to understand that it wasn't anything I had done, but rather their natural personalities, which meant I could adjust my focus to how to thrive with spirited children without guilt by creating routines and structures, natural consequence, or discipline plans, and opportunities for trips away from home to satisfy their thirst for adventure. And of course, there was always the mercy of a new day each morning.

Attending births as a doula highlighted each year. I attended two births in 2012, and a few in 2013, 2014, and 2015 before I closed the door on that profession. My last birth was my niece's in 2016. Though I thought a lot about my family while I was gone, it broke up the monotony of the days and weeks in the most amazing way.

Unlike my other babies, Amelia was sleeping well through the night by three months of age, and my energy was coming back. I was thinking about my garden, preparing for Daphney's birthday, and of course, working on lots of writing projects. We had just come back from our first week at camp; a Christian camp on a pond where you stay in an assigned cabin for a week. It would become an annual tradition for us; a Christmas present from my mom and stepdad. After a wonderful week surrounded by family, we returned home and I noticed for the first time that coming home felt so natural. This really WAS home.

Glen and I also got away for another date night that summer. We left the boys with his brother and the girls with my mom and rented a cabin within walking distance of the ocean. Despite having to pump milk to stay comfortable, it was a most enjoyable night; a reprieve from the rut I had found myself in.

The summer passed and September arrived, along with a flu that postponed the start of school, but once we began, Nemo in Kindergarten and Daphney in PreK, we found a steady rhythm of three days a week for lessons, one day for making Christmas gifts, and one day for running errands. In spare moments I worked on fall cleaning chores, decluttering, and switching over the seasonal clothes. I kept their few homeschool books on the bookshelf where the TV was held, and later, on a shelf in my room.

Nemo took a special trip on Amtrak's inaugural trip to Belfast with his Bompa and a family friend with connections. It would be the first of several such trips and his dreams of becoming a conductor were fostered. Glen went hunting around our property with his parents and brother in November, but no one got lucky. They still enjoyed the local hunters' breakfast with Nemo, Atlas, and Glen's grandfather. The photo of them that morning hung on our fridge for a long time.

Amelia remembers seeing photos of herself in her new highchair that autumn. After using a car seat on the couch and a playset with an upright seat as the only options to keep her off the floor, Glen made a chair for her to fit the bench seat at the table, using scrap wood at work. You would never know it was made so simply, however because it was an adorable chair with a rounded back and raised seat so she could easily eat with us. He drilled two holes in the back so a buckle (or belt) could be placed to keep her from climbing in and out of it. He modeled it after the pouting chair he grew up with, which had been made at the same wood manufacturing plant. Amelia would continue to use the chair sans buckle when she could climb in and out of it herself until she could no longer squeeze herself in. I was so bummed when I realized that the reason it went missing one day was that Glen had disposed of it in the fire pit, but we continued to enjoy the photos and stories.

While my focus remained on writing and doula work, that autumn I noticed that people were reaching out to me more often for help with home remedies. Making herbal products the year before made an impression on my community, and it became quite common to receive a call or text from someone needing help. I enjoyed that. It felt good to be useful to others and to feel like I could make a difference. It would be a few more years before I would embrace it as a vocation, but I continued to sell herbal remedies and support people as they requested help.

The winter arrived, and despite jokes the previous Christmas about it being our only yuletide in a camper, we were still there. As before, we put a full-size tree on the porch and decorated it with lights and ornaments. We enjoyed seeing the lights through the window from the living room. It was cozy, and it was peaceful. Hope remained. Many of my winter nights were spent using our new hot spot to research our family history, from which the early history of this book came. It was so hard to put it down at night, tracing our family lines, some back to Roman times, thanks to the hard work of other genealogists before me whose work I could build on. Somehow, despite all the challenges we had faced, and those yet to come, knowing we belonged to this family and were carrying on for older generations inspired and gave me hope for the future.

At the last count, reported by USA Today in 2006, over 180,000 families lived off the grid in the U.S.A. At the time, the number had increased by 33% each year for a decade. In 2011, it was estimated, using the 2000 census and a Texas A&M report that roughly 200,000 lived in an RV in one location (in other words, they weren't on vacation). As the number of these types of homes has clearly increased since then, some more recent estimates suggest over half a million families are living full time in an RV, parked indefinitely. How many of these are also off grid, and not just plugged in at a park or at their parent's house? It's difficult to say. People who live this way don't tend to be the type to stand up and say, "Hey, I'm over here! Come count me!" But we do know that the fastest-growing age bracket of RV dwellers is the 35-54 range, contrary to the previously held belief that RVing was for retired seniors, and news reports and blogs suggest that the top two reasons are economy and a thirst for adventure.

Though we don't know what the numbers are for sure, I can tell you that at the time of this writing, we have one other known off-grid house and two families in off-grid campers, just on our rural street. We also know multiple other people in our circle (excluding social media) who either live off-grid or in campers. And the surprising fact is that when we chose to do this adventure, we only knew of two couples who had attempted this, one of them several decades ago, and neither of them in a camper. It was something people did in the Carolinas or out west, not around here. I believe it is safe to say that the number of people building alternative lifestyles is indeed rising.

Why is this happening? Why are people who live in both rural and urban areas, of all income levels and many ages, choosing this unusual lifestyle over the comfort of flipping a switch and turning a faucet? The reasons vary widely, but I think they can be grouped into five basic concepts: one, as the number of people who move off-grid rises, resources, and education on how to do it becomes easier to access. YouTube and blogging have become empires of inspiration for the wannabe off gridder. Two, many of the people who choose this adventure cite environmental reasons for doing so. As an off gridder myself, I can tell you it is much harder to avoid using modern resources than it seems, even if you live off grid. Nonetheless, many find the idea of making a smaller carbon footprint motivational. Three, conservation, but for personal preference reasons. Smaller homes, fewer belongings, less clutter, more simplicity. Some people just want to let go of the modern trappings of America to bring more peace to their lives. Four, autonomy. These people often just want to be left the hell alone. They are the preppers. The ones who hold their neighbors at arm's length and definitely want the government to stay out of their business. Living off-grid means they aren't as dependent on the system for their resources. And finally, five, the group of off-gridders who left their last life behind for financial reasons. Maybe they were in a tight spot, or maybe they were tired of working two jobs or felt stuck in their job because of bills. I would dare say that the number of off gridders jumped when the housing bubble burst in 2009, the same one that landed us in a pickle.

A lot of people living off-grid would probably be able to pinpoint a specific reason that motivated them to take the leap, but I think we can also appreciate those who felt a piece of all of those reasons inside them. Our own situation was largely financial, but we also craved autonomy and simplicity. I always enjoyed the process of reusing and repurposing to avoid waste, and I sure did follow a lot of homesteading bloggers before we jumped! Just like the rest of our lives, the reasons we choose to move off-grid can be messy and complicated too.

The reasons people choose this lifestyle are varied, and so are the resulting homesteads. What exactly IS off grid? Technically, it means a building not connected to the power grid, but what it has come to mean as a lifestyle is so much more. Sometimes, people can't live entirely off the grid, but they do the best they can to meet their goals with what they have. Some may install a wood stove and stop relying on gas. Others get a well drilled and disconnect from town water. There are many "grids" that one can disconnect from in order to get closer to one's goal.

All of these things and more can be done in urban areas, depending on town codes. Many become known for replacing their pristine grass for garden boxes and growing their own food. Others raise small barnyard animals. Still, others choose to completely uproot themselves and start over on a plot of land in the middle of nowhere. That's what we did.

And yet, even our homestead setup is different from our neighbors. We try different methods, different tools, different approaches, and they both work, and it's even fun to see what new ways are dreamed up to accomplish similar goals. For example, one family may prefer to keep things as simple as possible and use kerosene lights in the evening, whereas we focused on building up our solar system to power electricity for lights and much more. Each family has a unique way of meeting their needs when it comes to water, waste disposal, refrigeration, cooking, heating, even construction (new, recycled, or old?) and internet (none, mobile hot spot, remote, cable, satellite?). There are literally countless variations of what it looks like to live off-grid, and therein lies much of its beauty: rather than live in a cookie-cutter house, paid for by a job you're stuck in, these off-grid homes become extensions of the families who live in them: what their goals are, what their resources are, what their skills and knowledge and experiences are, who they learned from, what their values and beliefs are. The home develops around the family in the most unique way.

The winter carried on. It was colder and brought with it more snow than the year before, but it was okay because we had our first year under our belt; `we knew we could get through another winter. Though the porch wasn't heated, it continued to provide a space for our snow gear, toys, tools, and music equipment, and we stayed warm inside thanks to the kerosene heater. As time went on, I grew more comfortable using it without fearing the worst thanks to all the horror stories of people not waking up in the morning. Autumn was often the worst emotionally, as we got used to it again and learned how to trust that our safety precautions would work, and each day I would relax a little more. We kept vents open a crack and would let the heater burn out briefly to clean the wick on a regular basis.

January came and went, and February arrived. The changing of the months brings hope that spring will be carried along with it and though we did not have the birth of a baby to look forward to, the unknown of the first year to keep us on our toes, or early spring to bring us relief, we continued to dream and make plans for all that we wanted to accomplish once warm weather arrived. But old man winter had other plans for us that changed everything.

There are a few dates I remember vividly. Our wedding, our birthdays, yes. Glen was laid off on December 10, 2010. We moved into our camper on May 5, 2011. We finally moved into our house on July 7, 2017, but on February 9, 2014, the blizzard named Nemo rocked our lives, and the date will thus forever be locked into the annals of my mind.

The satellite images of the storm as it careened up the east coast and through New England over a week's time were eerie. City lights blacked out. The air pressure dropped like a rock overnight in Maine. Swirling clouds angrily picked up speed. Thirty inches of snow dropped on us in a matter of hours; 40" a couple of states to our South. But it was the wind. It was the hurricane-force, 80 mph wind that scared the shit out of us and changed everything. The two of us, with our four young children, stranded in the middle of a field, with a 600' walk through the dark and furious blizzard to the closest safety of our vehicles, with no promise of a plowed road to lead us anywhere. So we spent a fitful night's sleep listening to the howling wind and snow pelting the walls, feeling it rock the camper, having the knowledge that the storm was supposed to worsen in the early morning.

My journal reveals that we were up by 4:30 am, "to the worst wind we had experienced here. The camper was shaking and the porch was grunting and creaking." The wind was getting stronger and Glen was getting antsy. It came in waves; there would be a lull, and then you would hear it coming as it raced up the hill behind and poured over us. Every time it slammed into the camper, Glen would jump out of bed and stare out into the darkness of our porch, where he could just make out the floating post that held up the middle of the porch, attached only to the roof. It was moving up and down a few inches at a time, up and down, with every gust of wind. In a short time, he gave up the idea of sleeping and instead paced back and forth in the kitchen.

The kids were still sleeping soundly, but every gust of wind left us holding our breath and planning our escape. "I've got to anchor it down, but how?" he would mutter. Eventually, he couldn't take it anymore and started bringing valuable belongings inside. By 5:30 am we had a system down. He would bring in a few things and I would find a place in the camper to stash them. All the while worrying that the porch would come loose from the ground.

Just before 6 am, Glen decided to use his comealong to attempt to anchor the center post to the underside of the camper, as it was now rising a foot in the air with every gust. We could tell, because there was a thermometer nailed to one side of the column. By now all of the kids except Nemo were at the table eating breakfast; I was trying to keep a normal morning routine with them to keep them calm, while helping Glen however I could. He went outside to work on the anchoring, but I could not comprehend then how dangerous this would be, or that I would soon fear I would never see him alive again.

I heard it coming. To this day, I get goosebumps when I think of how it felt, listening to that gust of wind, louder than any before it, come roaring up the mountain. I was so anxious for him, caught outside in the midst of the powerful blizzard. I held my breath.

The ripping, the shredding of wood. The most horrendous breaking, groaning, smashing sounds. Nothing compares to that moment when the sound filled my ears and body. He was still out there. I screamed out his name and pushed and shoved the door, but it wouldn't open. All I could imagine was that the porch had crashed down on top of him, blocking the door, and preventing me from getting to him. It was still so dark, I couldn't see through the window that looked into the porch to allay my fears. The kids began to scream and cry, and I feared the worst.

In what seemed like ages, but was really only seconds, Glen opened the door and walked in unscathed, and announced, "Well, it's gone." I could only see empty darkness behind him; no walls where the porch should be. Atlas started shaking violently from the shock of my response to the scare, and after we knew everyone was safe, I set to comforting the kids and myself at the same time.

We couldn't thoroughly evaluate the situation until sunrise, so we ate breakfast and drank coffee. The winds still swept through at 80 mph, smashing up against the debris of the addition and all of our belongings, but that was the last of the big gusts, and within a few hours, it had reduced to reasonable snowstorm-like behavior. Glen told me that he had been lying on his back next to the floating post when he heard the rumble and looked up to see the roof fly off, carrying the post with it. If that post had come back down and strayed from its original position... I am so thankful he is safe. Eighteen people died in that storm, and he easily could have been among the casualties.

When the sun rose enough that we could see through the swirling snow, the scene was surreal. Books, clothes, toys, Lego, craft supplies, littered all over the place. The table we had traded for the large one Glen built was missing a leg. My rocking chair, a gift at Nemo's birth, in pieces, half-buried in the snow. Suddenly, despite the reassurance that the dry snow would leave most things unharmed, I had a closer glimpse of what it would be like to lose your whole home to a natural disaster.

I cannot explain to you, the deep sadness I felt when looking over the yard, and seeing what the storm left us with. The porch, which my husband had so lovingly built for us, with what little money we had, while our babies bask in the sun on the floor; that porch, which had held our first Christmas tree on the homestead, many dinners at the table on summer evenings, and so many other memories, was smashed to pieces all over the yard.

Though we could not see the sun through the thick clouds and swirling snow, as soon as dawn broke Glen bundled up and stepped outside. One basket or box full at a time, he braced himself against the wind and lugged in most of our belongings. I dusted off the snow and either found a corner to stow them or handed them back so he could bring them to the storage camper. We moved at a fast pace until about 4:30 pm, after the kids had long grown anxious from being restricted in our room with the TV on, and Glen and I had no strength left.

Despite the horror, we managed to stay positive for most of the day. I did start feeling sick midday, from fatigue I think. And then I hit an emotional low shortly before we stopped working. I just couldn't face any more partially water-damaged belongings and ignore my babies any longer. It felt so unfair! We had worked so hard for how far we had gotten, and this was how the harsh earth took care of us?! Yet, we also could not ignore the miracles that found their way in: I did some sewing the night before and left my sewing machine inside. Glen brought his shotgun and guitar in right before it flipped. Glen remained uninjured. I wasn't outside. The camper itself sustained very minimal damage. Some of the building materials and most of our belongings went undamaged. We could rethink the location of the camper on our property, and our tax return had just come. Things could have been far worse. We even saw the sun peeking through the clouds before it set that night. It would be spring next month.

The adrenaline of that day helped us to get things taken care of the best we could, without feeling completely overwhelmed, but the real test was yet to come. It would be another four months before the last pieces of debris were finally picked up. It was a long and discouraging process, not just because of the initial loss and terror, but because it was lost time, and our living space, for an unforeseeable length of time, was cut in half.

After the shock of Blizzard Nemo, and the initial cleanup, assisted by Glen's parents and his brother and sister-in-law, we fell back into a routine as best we could. One of the most pressing struggles was now keeping the chickens safe. When the roof blew off the porch, it smashed into the chicken run and broke the fencing, but no matter how many holes we threw a patch on, raccoon and other creatures seemed to find a way in. There were just too many pieces of debris to be able to see the damage to the coop, and with all the snow, no good way to move it. After one young hen lost an eye during a raccoon attack one night but decided to fight for her life, we blocked the entrance from the coop to the run after sunset, and just let them out during the day. We doctored the hen back to health with some herbal assistance, she was named Buttercup, and she became a favorite pet until her death a few years later.

Raccoon became a bad word around our homestead. Between eating chickens, chicken feed, and making a mess of the trash, they became regular targets for our shotgun. The end of winter was an especially trying season each year, as the long drought of easy food seamed to drive them from the woods to our yard. One day in March, I put Amelia down for a nap and the other kids helped me to pick up trash the raccoons had spread around. We got it all except the diapers that had frozen to the ice, and Glen was happy to return home and find that all he needed to do was take a trip to the dump.

Though I was able to attend another birth, that spring was really hard. The porch incident left us discouraged, the fridge was not cooperating after days of letting it sit, and there was less snow to keep things cold in the cooler. Then Amelia started cutting molars and she and I did not sleep well for weeks, I was having to get up and tend to two exhausting young children and another who needed his school lessons. I began struggling emotionally again. We needed spring to come already! We had an abundance of rain that spring, and the snow finally melted enough that the kids could go out for more time each day.

In May, Glen started repurposing materials from the porch to build a permanent shed behind where the house would be built. Amazingly, the storm windows had not broken, so he used those too. It was 12x8, two stories high, with four windows and a ladder to the second story. The first floor had makeshift shelving units made from materials being thrown away at his workplace, and there was plenty of room for plastic totes, and bags could be hung from the joists. In this way, we were able to move our belongings from the storage camper to something actually built for the homestead, and later that year we found a new home for the old thing.

Meanwhile, we moved the garden boxes from behind the damaged chicken coop and set them up by the new shed. I lost track of the number of pails of dirt I moved from the foundation site's freshly dug soil to the new garden, but I got it done.

Spring cleaning in the camper and yard work getting done rejuvenated where the winter wore us down. It felt good to be active and doing something to improve the homestead, even if it was not as much as we had hoped to accomplish. We took loads of junk to the dump, and with every trip, our spirits improved.

My sister was looking for a place to stay and had intended to come camp out in our yard in trade for childcare help, so we set up a platform for her tent. When that didn't work out, she spent a few Saturdays babysitting for me so I could focus on gardening and yard work instead of childcare. Every bit helped, and an extra set of hands was priceless! In June, we also took a trip to the York Zoo with Glen's family and took lots of pictures of the kids interacting with the animals.

Father's Day arrived, and I was finally able to enact my secret plan. The kids and I decorated a poster board with handprints and drawings that said, "Happy Father's Day to the World's Best Papa" in big letters. On the Friday before Father's Day, we drove to his work and arrived shortly before the bell rang, announcing the end of the workday. As employees exited, they stopped to read the sign we proudly held high, until he came through the door. He was so happy. It went off perfectly. And the sign still hangs in the shed today.

~~~~~

Two years. Two years had passed. We were still in the camper, and even though it felt like we were moving one step forward, two steps back some days, every season somehow brought us closer to our goal.

Would it work out? Would we build our off grid-house? That was still the plan, and time would tell. We could truly only take things as they came and hold on for the ride. If the past year had taught us anything, it was that you can't truly prepare for everything, but you can still aim the bow of your ship, interlock arms, and hold your head high. So, we did just that.

Chapter Four

~Home~

In our early days of marriage, I read quite a few books on being a good wife and creating a godly home. I was 18, wounded, and had no idea what I was doing, but my heart was in the right place. I have looked back on those days and called myself lazy, because I didn't keep up on the chores consistently, instead doing lots of reading and writing, having used the excuse that our home was a never-ending construction site. With time I have come to understand that it was a season I needed, of rest and reflection, following a very difficult season. I am grateful for those two years in transition of learning to be a wife, and to run my own home before I brought children into the world. Reading all of those books was a memorable part of the process. Sometimes these books were controversial, as in "Created To Be His Helpmeet" by Debi Pearl, or as classic as Edith Shaeffer's, "The Hidden Art of Homemaking." I'm sure most of them I found by chance on Amazon.

Out of all the books I read, one story in one of the volumes, whose title I cannot recall, stuck out to me and began to shape my actions. It was a story about a woman who visited a poor wife. She lived in an old house in serious need of repair. The visitor wrote that when she was invited to other homes, she would often be offered desserts and coffee or other elaborate things, but in this home, this poor woman offered her tea and homemade bread with preserves. What struck her as so unique and warming about this encounter was how this woman, despite her obviously unfortunate circumstances, had a big smile on her face, and unashamedly welcomed her visitors into her quaint home and offered them what she had. Did she feel shame inwardly? If she did, it did not show. The visitor later wrote a book on homemaking and included interviews with homemakers. She wrote that this particular woman made her feel more loved than any other hostess.

I knew at that moment, that that was the woman I wanted to be. No matter whether my house was under construction, or years later, if I lived in a camper, I wanted my guests to feel welcome and loved. And interlaced with our journey to adapt to our new space and make the most of it, was a desire to make our home hospitable, no matter it's size.

My grandmother shared some of her memories of our experiences, and I was so grateful, that tucked in the middle was this statement, "There was always an offer of a cup of coffee, when we might visit from time to time. We would be shown the most recent invention that Glen would be working on and the children wanted to show us their latest Lego projects, etc." This was the prize! The winning ticket! Every once in awhile a friend will say something about feeling welcome in our home. That despite the ongoing construction that seems to be our life's story, there is always a cup of tea, and the aromatherapy diffuser, music, or other accommodations to make them feel welcome. The other piece of this that I feel is so crucial is one's attitude. The lady in the story smiled, and through the story's telling, I could imagine that she listened intently and respectfully to her guests, making eye contact and giving them her genuine attention and care. When someone does this for you, it's harder to notice what might be lacking in the environment, because it is made up of the love felt by the company. My friends have remarked on the attention I give them, saying it feels like they are all that matter when we visit. I would daresay, love can cover up a multitude of things; not just sins!

This feels like success to me, because I have been married for 16 years now and have yet to live in a finished home. The carpenter's house is never done, right? I know that I can't wait for a finished house to have the perfect place to welcome guests, because who knows how many years I would have to wait, and how many opportunities to host would have passed by then! Despite the situation, I want to carve out space in our home that makes our guests feel comfortable, and it is a gift when I hear that they did.

As part of my journey to accept the home I live in (skipping ahead in this story a little bit), I read a book in 2015 called Love the Home You Have, by Melissa Michaels. Inspired by this book, I wrote a purpose statement for our home. I didn't print it out and hang it on the wall, but it is saved in a journal, and now I'll share it with you.

"Our home is where our family spends its days; working, resting, learning, and playing. It is a safe space for us to be ourselves and be loved, where we are refreshed in body, mind, and spirit, where we can fulfill our personal purposes, and where we can offer a peaceful retreat to guests."

I hope always to pursue this path.

After just over a year of living in the camper it finally felt like home, but in 2013 we began to feel more outward-focused. We had settled in, it was now our home, so we could move forward with plans for the future. After the snow melted and cleanup work from the blizzard had been completed, we did move the camper to the front side of the site dug out for the house foundation. Here we hoped to be safely farther away from the old trees that might fall during storms. We moved some of the old dock sections we had used for various projects, and set them up as a deck, with some old fencing to the front and one side. We got such a kick out of the fact that those same dock sections, that we had gotten secondhand, had served so many purposes. I also started flower boxes in front of the deck and grew marigolds, morning glories, nasturtiums, and a few other pretty things. After getting fed up with cleaning up trash that the raccoons had made a mess of, I started building a wooden dumpster. I had been on Glen's case about building one but finally got tired enough of waiting that I created a plan for one myself. After starting the project with leftover materials, Glen gave me some helpful advice, and I created a very sturdy container that has kept animals out to this day. There was also a barrel sitting on the porch by the window at the table, and our new friend Buttercup, the hen that had lost an eye to a raccoon, took up this spot as her perch. Nemo would see her through the window and come out to say hello. She loved the attention he gave her. In fact, all the hens loved this little porch!

Another little hangout that we created, before moving the camper, was by the new shed, now filled with all our belongings from the old camper and the destroyed addition. Glen attached a piece of trim about halfway up the face of the second floor and from giant hooks screwed into it, stretched out a large tarp using metal poles buried in the ground twenty feet out. Underneath, we put more fencing around the perimeter and a table and chairs within. What it created was a covered area where we could hang out, with a psychological boundary for the kids that encouraged them to play underneath it where I could keep my eyes on them. Nemo even set up his Thomas trains on the table, using dirt and rocks to fill out the layout.

Next to the shed, Glen built a large swing set with one wooden swing that had come from the old house, and a tire swing, both of which hung from ropes and lasted a few years before needing to be replaced, because the holes had worn out on the seats. Glen had hoped to build a fort onto the side of it, but while that didn't happen, it did end up with a makeshift slide and a basketball hoop attached, all of which continued to provide the kids with lots of fun for several years.

This area, around the shed, the swings, the garden, and a fire ring, became the party central when we hosted our first "big birthday bash" to celebrate Nemo's 7th, Daphney's 5th, and Atlas' 3rd birthdays (that year Amelia got her own party to mark her first birthday). This became a tradition for five years, in which a large group of family and friends would join us on the last Saturday in June to celebrate all of our children's birthdays, and we would go all out on food, party favors, music, tents, games, and other special details. This first year, it had rained the day before, and though we did not have to cancel, children did go home covered in mud! The puddles were glorious that day, and the mud was the center of attention. With party music in the background, hot dogs being passed out, adults chatting and kids splashing, it was a memorable time that we later made into a video we posted on YouTube.

This was also the summer we made friends with another Christian, homeschooling family who lived on the next road over. We had been introduced by mutual friends years before, and after we reconnected at the post office of all places, we began visiting at least every other week. We had playdates, went on field trips together, had family dinners, went hiking, and even traded kids regularly so us moms could have some time to ourselves. Neither of us had other close friends at the time, so this was invaluable to us both. Unfortunately, a few years later we went separate ways because she was not able to reconcile with our differences in parenting; a very sad time that took months for the kids and me to recover from, but we still appreciate the time we had together while it lasted. We needed friends, and by the time we parted ways, we had made new friends elsewhere. We were grateful that God took care of our needs and we were never alone.

Speaking of never being alone, one of the most commonly asked questions we've had was, how do you find space to be alone? Truth be told, that is a hard one to answer when you have four children in less than six years time. Even if a mother had all the space in the world, her young children would still be tied tightly to her apron strings! I'm not sure how things would have looked as the kids got older had we still been in the camper. When they were young, they needed a lot of supervision, and by the time they were old enough to leave so Glen and I could take evening walks by ourselves, it was getting quite cramped at home. Not just for lack of privacy, but literally cramped. They were getting so big, and needing space to keep their personal belongings safe, as well as time alone. But in 2013, they were still small and we made it work. Balancing our needs for privacy and space, with our desire to be together as a family sometimes worked really well and other times not so much. Some days we could escape to our rooms, with the obligatory, "I'm going to bed, please leave me alone," but some days; a desire for peace and quiet necessitated eating my lunch in the car, or taking an extra walk to the mailbox, hoping no one was trailing behind. And this applied just as much to the kids and Glen as it did to me! Knowing he would not likely have any peace and quiet at home, Glen would often sit in the car at the end of the driveway after work and just breathe, preparing for all of the stories the kids would lovingly bombard him with on his arrival. I guess in the end, balancing our needs for privacy was a challenge, but we worked through it, and one way or the other our needs were mostly met. It also was a valuable lesson in character; to respect others' needs to be left alone at times. After spending their whole lives sleeping right next to each other, Atlas and Amelia, as well as the older two to some extent, do not like sleeping in a room by themselves. They much prefer the company of a sibling, and I think, given many of today's social issues, with families falling apart, their closeness is a special gift, even if they quickly switch from being best friends to enemies at the drop of a hat! Such is the life of siblings.

My growing skills as an herbalist continued to be challenged. In July, as friends of ours were leaving one evening, Atlas tripped and fell against the fire ring. One hand was badly burned. Much of it looked like a second-degree burn, but there was a small section on his palm where the top layer of skin was completely gone.

We didn't have a pediatrician yet, and I didn't want to wait hours in the ER for cream and a bandage, so I gave him Tylenol and a chilled compress of comfrey infusion, and then wrapped his hand in profuse amounts of honey, held on with gauze and plastic wrap. We alternated these treatments for a few days, and then when the skin began to visibly heal, I switched to an herbal salve. Within two weeks it had almost completely healed, and his hand never scarred. He never showed any signs of infection, and as concerned and alert as I was throughout the process, looking for signs of danger, he healed quickly and completely, and my confidence in natural medicine continued to grow.

Also this year, I would have another decent opportunity to decide whether I had the skills and knowledge to handle a minor emergency. From what I understand, the kids were trying to help their two year old sister up into the bunk bed when she slipped and fell. She landed on a pile of toys and made a one inch gash on the top of her cheekbone. Blood was pouring from the wound, or so it felt. After briefly putting compression on the wound and then releasing it to get a better look, it actually squirted out for a split second. Her siblings cried out and Nemo asked if she was going to see Jesus. When Glen wouldn't answer his phone, I called the office and had him summoned over the loudspeaker. I knew head wounds bleed a lot, but I wanted reassurance about what the right decisions to make were. The bleeding came back under control with continued pressure, so I waited for him to come home and see it so I could have a second opinion. We decided to butterfly bandage it, and it actually healed very well. I applied a healing salve, and to this day she has only a small, faint scar. I am so thankful that whatever she landed on did not hit her eye!

Thinking ahead to winter, Glen used patio bricks to build a hearth and he installed a camp wood stove so we would not have to rely entirely on kerosene for heating. Having grown up with wood heat, this made me far more comfortable. He also moved the RV water tank from under the couch and rebuilt it so the whole seating area could be pushed farther from the stove. The couch became a bench, built into the wall under the window, with the original cushioned seat portion sitting on top, and the tank was set upright on end, between the couch and the stove, with a wood trimmed-out box around it and a removable shelf to give access to the pipes underneath. Next, he made a heat shield out of metal roofing and wrapped it around the new water tank cabinet and behind the stove. The YouTube video Glen made about it generated more views than the rest of our videos, as well as the most opinionated comments.

When the woodstove was moved in, the standalone bookshelf that sat in that spot and held the TV was moved out. Glen next moved to the master bedroom where he removed two of the cabinets and built shelves that wrapped around the room, even across the windows, creating ample storage space for all of our homeschool books, craft projects, the TV, and much more.

That year, two years after moving out of our house, the foreclosure was finalized. It was such an odd sense of closure that came with that knowledge. We had known we weren't going back. The bank had long ago changed the locks, and we were stubborn; we were going forward not backward. Yet this news made our decision all the more final. It didn't belong to us anymore. The house or the decision. It was a done deal.

To make matters more strange, the house was then put on auction and sold for less than 20% of what we owed on it. It sat empty for a while, which was sad to see when we would occasionally drive by, but eventually, another family moved in. That felt better. Our house would be loved again.

It felt ironic that in the same season we began feeling the need to remodel our camper and fluff the rest up a bit, that our old house officially became someone else's. It was a reminder that it was indeed time to aim the ship out to sea and to stop looking backward. It was time to remember what our adventure was all about, and to create the contentment we were looking for, right where we were.

On our 20 acres of family land, our homestead is planted toward the back end, away from the road, and surrounded by trees. When Glen's parents took ownership, there was a field, once maintained, that wrapped from the road, up and around a corner, and behind some trees. As you follow the field around the corner, it goes uphill, as our property is on the backside of a small mountain. The field is maintained once again by Glen's parents and our eldest son, with trees going all around. There are a few new neighbors building around us, but vision of each other's homes is obstructed, protecting our privacy; just the way we like it.

It was about this time in our story that the cousin's family whom our acreage came from decided that they did not want the adjacent 27 acres, so they put it on the market. Land is not cheap in our town, so when it didn't sell quickly, the owners decided to hire a logging crew, who cut down a large number of their trees.

We could see a lot of the activity happening on the other side of our tree line, and our eldest child, Nemo was highly disturbed. "They are killing the trees!" He paced the edge of the field, stomping back and forth, giving the crew the stink eye, even though they were too far away to see. He was seven years old, but he was faced with a large moral issue for his little heart, and no matter how many times we explained that it was healthy for the younger trees because it gave them more room to grow and light to make food, it was a relief when they left so Nemo could put his guard down.

Hiking around the property line was fun. I had been taking the kids through a course on what to do in emergency situations, including being lost in the woods. As we trudged through the woods, we looked for safe sources of drinking water, dry areas for building shelters, and materials that would keep you warm. They were still young, but it was good food for thought, and we enjoyed the hike as a family; exploring the unused acreage of our little mountain.

The kids grew bigger and we continued to spend as much time in the great outdoors as we could. Despite my seasonal depression, I had a great appreciation for the blessings in my life, for our big family, our plumb line of values, and the compass that was our world view. We did everything as a family, talked about everything as a family, and supported each other's visions as a family. We had each other's backs. Even when frustrating things happened, we always knew there was a way through. We might have to make up a path as we went along, but whatever happened, we were together, so we had all that we needed.

What things do you take for granted in your house? Sure, you might go to thoughts about technology, or perhaps a garage if you have one, but what about a house that is level? Okay, if you have a farmhouse that probably didn't come to mind. How about doorknobs? Or windows bigger than two feet wide, that don't need a crank to open them? A fridge that runs more than six weeks in a row? How about room for a trash can? Or a place to put your shoes? Can you take a 15 minute hot shower? How about a house that doesn't vibrate and shake every time there is a storm? Do you have a washer and dryer? Light switches that work every time you flip them? I don't know about you, but these are some of the things that we took for granted when we lived in our old house on the grid.

We knew we were giving them up temporarily when we moved into our camper, but it wasn't until we lived without them that we realized how valuable these modern blessings are. And it is this same experience that taught us appreciation and gratefulness for the blessings we still had. As we built our house and installed real bedroom doors, unlike the curtains that hung over our doorways in the camper, cheers erupted from all. Yes, it was exciting to see our house coming together, but it was living without these things for six years that made us realize that it is the simple things we take for granted that can make some of the biggest differences in our lives.

Talking to a friend who was moving off-grid into a camper, she said that was one aspect she was looking forward to learning, even the hard way because she admired the way we talked about all the things we valued in our new house. She knew that though it would be a long journey, living in an off-grid tiny home would teach her family valuable life lessons, and draw them closer together. This family is in their fourth year of camper living and still going strong.

Late summer for homesteaders means, you guessed it! Canning! Our garden produced abundant vegetables that summer of 2013, so I did a lot of canning in our camper. I even made a video for our YouTube channel all about canning in a small space. Each step has to be carefully planned, and as much prep work done ahead of time as possible.

The whole kitchen had to be cleaned of course, but each step of canning had to be cleaned up from before I could continue, in order to make room for the next step. Wash and sterilize the jars, clean up. Cut up the veggies and pack the jars, clean up. Put them in the canner, clean up. Set the jars out to cool, clean up. The seven-quart canner was so huge that I could just barely fit it on the stove below the hood, and I certainly couldn't fit it under the sink faucet. The fastest way to fill it was to connect it directly to the filtered water coming through the 12-volt pump on a 165-gallon tank of dug well water outside. And lug it in, I did! Canning was very rewarding though, and we had some produce last through the whole winter thanks to our amazing crop that year. Ironically, that was also our last garden of that size to this date.

Autumn arrived, and with it another difficult life season. Not the least of which included 18 month old Amelia cutting more molars. Up until then she had been a great sleeper, spending part of each night in her own bed, then in ours, and always waking up with a smile on her face. But those molars were mean son-of-a-guns, and nothing would keep her from crying at night, even as I tried to rock her on the couch at all hours, praying for enough energy and patience to get through our school lessons in the morning. One night, for the very first time in my mothering career, I actually took her for a drive to get her to be quiet, so at least everyone else could sleep. I don't remember it being very successful and never tried again.

November brought with it the beginning of the worst. Over the next three months, we lost 16 people we either knew personally or directly through someone we knew personally. Some of them were older and their time had come, but others were young, and their deaths were unfair. It was a very difficult season emotionally. I hated it when the phone rang. My heart would drop because I just knew it would be the news of someone else passing. In January, Nemo had a panic attack, thinking I was going to die. We attended funerals and cried and prayed, and waited for the season to end. I wrote in my journal, "what the freaking hell is going on?!" We were all very confused and distraught. And in the middle of this nightmare, our life at home was made yet more complicated by the weather.

In January, we repeatedly had nights dipping 20 degrees below zero. The floors were so cold we would throw our blankets down to walk on them so our feet would stay warm. It reminded me of a bohemian caravan. Daphney says it was cozy, and she remembers eating chicken pie on one of those days.

The bedroom windows would no longer hold a tight seal around the frame, so after learning the hard way one storm, we shoved bath towels in the cracks to keep snow from blowing in. I would work all day, it felt like, to thaw out the pipes using heat directed with a fan from the radiant kerosene heater (which took up precious hall space) and hot water packs, to scramble to wash all the dishes, just to have it freeze all over again, sometimes before the day was done. I wondered what the point was of even trying to thaw the pipes some days, and this frustration was only amplified on the nearly daily occurrence in which I found mouse poop all through the kitchen drawers, despite multiple traps being set, and I would have to wash everything again. My journal became a place for me to vent my fatigue and frustration about "stupid homestead stuff." It was a long winter, made only more difficult by the fact that I was already done and needed out.

The wind blew hard that winter. Sitting in our new spot in front of the house site, we were safe from the old trees that might fall over, but we got the full force of the wind instead. Some storms, we would sit on the couch and watch the opposite wall swell inward with gusts, wondering how strong a wind it would have to be to blow us over. Our Google searches were a bit eerie those nights. Kind of like looking up your symptoms and diagnosing yourself with cancer. A word from the wise, if you live in a camper, don't do that.

One night we were supposed to get a real doozy of a storm, with high winds. Having already been traumatized, and knowing we wouldn't sleep at all, we packed up our bags and slept at Glen's parents', reassured to discover the next morning that the camper was right where we left it. On at least one other occasion we just rolled out the blankets for kids to sleep on the floor and had shoes lined up by the door, quite sure we wouldn't need them, but more at peace with an escape plan.

In the midst of this weather, we tested our new wind turbine, which Glen installed during the fall before the ground froze over. He ordered the kit online for about $500, and purchased galvanized pipe, cables, a bucket, and cement, and erected the thing behind the camper. When the wind blew we would watch the gauges showing incoming power and the battery power level. Our hope was that during days when we didn't get enough solar power, the wind turbine would pick up the slack, but even though the wind would blow and that sucker would spin so hard it made a racket and looked like it was going to fly off and hit a neighbor's house, it never charged the batteries. It was a complete disappointment and we laughed when the following winter, a cable snapped, the pipe broke, and the turbine came crashing down. Good riddance.

February finally arrived. The month before spring starts, and we needed fresh hope. I was anxious for our newest nephew to be born, selfishly because I wanted to celebrate life instead of marking another death. We needed something wonderful to happen. And wonderful did. After a very long and difficult labor, he was finally born. We all shed tears of joy, expressed gratefulness, and believed this was the turning point. Things should get easier now. But that wasn't to be.

Three days later, my mom was in the hospital. By a sheer accident, she was kicked in the face by one of her horses, shattering her jaw. It was a miracle she survived, and that she retained as much of the structure and function of her body that she did, but it would be a long, uphill battle that she has still not fully healed from. I have lost count of how many surgeries she has had, and she spent a couple of weeks in the hospital, and then about two months with her jaw wired shut. She is a fighter, and my respect for her grew even more through that experience.

That's hindsight though. At the moment, it was one of the worst things I had ever faced. My kids were sick, and storm after storm hit, and I was only able to visit her a few times in the hospital. I am grateful my sister could be there more often. One night, my mom called me from her hospital bed. It must have been around 11 pm. She whispered that she wanted to hear me sing. She was in so much pain. She didn't say so, but I knew she must be, for her to call me like that. Today, she doesn't remember that call. I wanted to drive out to her, but we were in the middle of another storm, and I didn't even know if I could get my car out of the driveway if I trudged the 700' or so through the snow to the car. I was desperately tempted to try.

During one of her multiple surgeries, I was waiting on a call from my sister to hear any news while I was baking a birthday cake for Atlas. Amelia, then almost two years old, decided to dump a bottle of nail polish remover into the batter, and I had to start all over again. In the midst of pain and turmoil was life, and cake batter with nail polish remover.

God watched over her and the surgeries were a success. All too soon she was back to work (before the wires were even removed!) and she fought her way to her new life, post-accident.

We needed spring to come so badly.

Our tax return arrived, and we added that to our savings, bringing us to just over $10,000. Glen was hired for a new position at work, which came with a $4 per hour raise. We set a goal to get the foundation poured that summer and be in by the fall of 2016. Two and a half years. Despite a major setback that would happen later in the year, which would cause me to question our building plans entirely, our actual timeline until moving in would only be a little more than three years away. The planner in me would love to have known that!

Somehow, despite the trauma and hardship experienced through the winter, Glen had an idea for a business plan. I think he needed this idea as a way of feeling hopeful and having a hobby. His whole life, Glen has prided himself on coming up with new ideas. If you're familiar with the Gallop Strengths Finder, it wouldn't surprise you to know that his #1 strength is Ideation. We call him the ideas guy, it's just what he does. This particular winter, he began brewing over an idea about a new kind of bag. It would be a modernized hobo bag. Imagine the old image seen in movies, of a traveler, hitching rides on trains, carrying a sack tied to a stick over his shoulder. Except instead of any old stick, and an old rag or kerchief, it's a stylish bag made with a machined out and molded bamboo or oak stick, and denim, leather, canvas, or other high quality cloth bag.

Glen bought himself a sewing machine, made regular trips to town for cloth, and began sewing on the table in the camper. Before we knew it, he had piles of identical bags of various styles. He registered as a business with the state, purchased a tent, a table, and other equipment he would need, and that summer we would travel to different fairs in Maine, selling Bags on Sticks.

Some days were more profitable than others, but eventually, Glen decided it was not worth the time. People loved the bags, but not enough to buy many of them. Next, he began selling them at consignment shops. Some sold, but he just didn't have a strong enough hold in the marketing department. The most exciting moment came when a popular online opinion site wrote a satire piece and mentioned his website. The views skyrocketed, but sales did not follow. Most sales came from Etsy, usually 1-4 bags a month. Eventually, Glen decided it was time to put his energy elsewhere, closed the business, and gave away most of the remaining inventory. It was sad, partly because we lost valuable money while trying to save for a house, and partly because the ideas guy needed a success, but the great thing about Glen is that the ideas keep coming. Since then, he has been working on another business plan that he hasn't entirely given up on yet. We'll see where it goes!

With warm weather arriving in the spring of 2014, wildlife came out of hibernation and started looking for food. One morning I heard the chickens squawking and looked out to discover a huge bobcat pouncing around on top of the chicken run! All of the chickens were running around panicked, except for Buttercup, the beloved hen who had already had a face-to-face encounter with a raccoon and apparently felt confident enough to sit there and watch the predator with curiosity. By the time I got outside with a handgun, it had already wandered off. We stuck close to the house that day!

Warm weather arrived none too soon, and with it, plans to begin construction on our house, finally. The kids were getting bigger, the camper was aging from overuse, and we had all lost our excitement for this adventure in tiny home living. We had saved up enough money to begin our search for a crew who could come in and pour us a foundation for our house. We had no idea that such a search would be so difficult, or that it would set us back a year and almost drive us to move elsewhere, but this spring, we agreed that it was time to begin our efforts to transform our savings into our forever home – a house that no one, not even a bank could take from us. There is a quote by an unknown author that says: "You don't have to have it all figured out to move forward… just take the next step." How true a statement for us at that moment in time. We did not pretend to know where the path might lead us, but it was time to take another step.

Chapter Five

~Small Stones~

I remember the first email, though I don't remember when it came. It was a scout for the National Geographic. They wanted to know if we were interested in being featured on a TV show they were developing about families who live off-grid. They had found our blog and YouTube channel and thought our family might be a good fit.

Multiple emails and phone calls ensued as Glen and I played around with the idea of having our story on cable TV. What would that be like? How would it benefit us? Would it possibly help us to get our house built faster? They did want to be there when the walls went up. We seemed like a good fit; much of our produce came from our garden, we were off-grid, in a rural area, and I homeschooled the kids… but then there was a problem. "Your husband works outside the home? You mean you get your income from somewhere other than your homestead?" Essentially, it disqualified us. They were interested enough to ask how much money they would have to pay us for it to be worth Glen staying home during the production of the episodes, but definitely weren't biting at replacing his income. That also begged the question, if they were willing to pay us so Glen would stay home, would that just be for appearances so the audience would think we lived off our homestead alone? Had they accepted similar offers by other featured guests?

In order to be on the show, Glen would lose money, and we would be living with a group of strangers camped in our yard for several weeks, a couple of times, just to get a highly edited snapshot of our story on TV. Nope. Not happening. We turned down subsequent offers from Discover, BBC, TLC, and a couple of others. I responded to the first few emails, telling them upfront we weren't interested because of what happened the first time, but then I just started deleting them.

It wasn't just the high expectations they set that disappointed us, it was the difference we knew that existed between reality and what they showed on similar programs. Off-grid shows drastically misrepresent what it's really like; accentuating the glory, and making hardship look like fun. How can they possibly explain it with a one hour, or a few half-hour episodes? They'll show the most exciting, most attractive aspects, or maybe even problems that get resolved, but the day-to-day, season-to-season drudgery? The emotional breakdowns? The dull work that keeps the homestead running? No, these shows incredibly under-represent, and they are why people with two incomes, giant houses, and new cars create Pinterest boards of their dream houses out in the woods and talk about living off the land. They just have no idea what they are talking about. The media's efforts at making money off of helping homesteaders represent, sadly result in distancing people from reality.

Then, of course, there is the problem that occurs when you live such a lifestyle, and your loved ones watch reality TV. The result is one of my biggest pet peeves.

"Oh! Have you seen ___ show? They can all of their food!"

"Good for them."

"But they have to collect all of their water from rain barrels first."

"Okay."

"And they have super cold winters and have to heat with wood."

"Do you know where we live?"

"Yes, but they don't have electricity and had to lug in all their supplies using four-wheelers."

(Under my breath) "Good lord, where have you been?"

Basically, no matter how many times we talked about our life, how we had to lug all of our water with wagons and sleds, filter groundwater, design our own solar system, empty compost toilets twice a week at least (as in, a bucket of poop), and clean kerosene filers so we don't die of noxious fumes, canned our own home-grown produce and built many of our homestead buildings using repurposed or carefully purchased materials, doctored our injured chickens, and myriad other projects and chores that would make for great entertainment… it's never good enough now.

Once someone has it in their head that they know what homesteading is all about because they saw some 20 minute show, they can't hear us when we say, "Yes, we live like that." It's always, "yeah, but…" and then they're telling another story that we are all too familiar with. Not only did we have to persevere through hardship, and do it without community, we had to listen to people disregard our story because they didn't see it on TV. Truthfully, it would feel hurtful if we didn't know how to just let it go. Even better, were the comments suggesting we should watch these shows because they live like us. As if we would enjoy watching someone else clean off solar panels covered in snow, lug propane tanks around, or hang their laundry on the clothesline because that's what we do! That would be like watching a YouTube video with pretty music featuring someone washing dishes. Fascinating.

You might think I'm being a little harsh about this. I know people mean well, and I accept it as that, but I damn well know about unburying firewood in the middle of a storm, and I don't need to watch someone refilling their water tanks any more than you want to watch someone mow the lawn. In the end, I decided I really didn't feel like putting my family through the difficulty of being in a TV show only to add to the plethora of media representing homesteaders. At least with our blog and YouTube channel, our story wasn't getting censored by anyone else, though I was fully aware that it also was incomplete.

His alarm goes off on his cell phone, on the shelf above his head, and I roll over onto my other side. I sleep on the side of the bed closest to the door, so I can tend to children through the night, so now he climbs over me to get out of our bed and stand on the one-foot by four-foot section of floor between our bed and the other side of our room, the only floor space that room had, grabbing his clean clothes from one of the many shelves surrounding our bed as he gets down. He gets dressed, grateful that the winter is ending, and he doesn't need quite so many layers, and he doesn't need to get up early enough to snow blow the driveway. Instead, he throws on some clothes, grabs his coffee cup, his phone, wallet, a utility knife, and a few assorted screws he transferred from yesterday's pants to today's and, after kissing me, heads out the door. I can hear him switching the propane tanks outside. We're almost empty, so he'll fill the second tank at the hardware store on his way home from work. I think he emptied the toilet last night, so that should be all set.

Another half hour goes by, and my alarm goes off. I drag myself out of bed after another night dealing with a child's upset belly and make myself some breakfast. It won't be long before the kids wake up, so I try to get some journaling time in on our couch, tiny but cozy with its pillows, and I write. When the kids wake up, I'll go tend to the chickens, and on my way back in I will bring the five-gallon jugs of water from the car that we collected at Glen's parents' yesterday, so I can refill our drinking water dispenser, which is running low. I'll make the kids their daily bagels with cream cheese, using the wire toaster set on top of the stove, and then I'll clean breakfast off the table, putting the used napkins in the plastic grocery bag hanging on the bathroom doorknob that holds trash, to make room for morning lessons before they go outside to play, no doubt returning covered in mud. And so begins a typical spring day in our neck of the woods.

Our goals for 2014 were pretty simple and straightforward: keep responsibilities as low as possible so we can focus on one thing – building the house. Though I would begin babysitting our baby nephew in the fall, and each school year until he was in preschool, this year I would avoid gardening (though it opened me up to criticism on the blog), I stopped writing a manuscript I was working on for an herbal book, and in May I journaled, "AFN's days are numbered." I transitioned my blog to an easier to maintain Facebook page, and closed down the blog that summer, moving my focus to the house and my doula service. I had several potential clients, and I felt it would take less of my attention given that attending births was not part of my regular schedule. I completed a Hypnobirth doula training, and later on planned a parenting class. Yet my desire to grow my doula service too was winding down, as it interfered with family's needs, and emotionally I was still struggling to understand that it was okay for me to have a side job. On the weekends, I supported Glen as we attended fairs to sell his Bags on Sticks, or to bring them to consignment shops. I actively advertised and sold our chicken eggs. We had hope that as we looked for the right company to help us put in our foundation, we would continue to add funds to our savings.

Meanwhile, our concerns about the kids' health began to rise. We were beginning to realize that Daphney, at age five, had Celiac Disease, and that after a really bad case of bronchitis, Atlas, at age four, now had cough-variant asthma. We began changing our diet as a family to accommodate their needs, and experimented with various herbal products to reduce their, at times, disconcerting symptoms, which we were afraid was only made worse by living in such close quarters for so long, constantly exposed to the mold that grew back as quickly as we destroyed it. On top of that, I had an early miscarriage in July. I named her Maebh (pronounced Mave), which means cause of great joy. Feeling overwhelmed by stress and showing physical symptoms of it, camp was much needed in August, and our vision became crystal clear: get that house built and get out of the camper. We would begin making calls to concrete crews when we returned from camp.

What we were attempting to do seemed crazy. Though our talk of living off grid garnered responses about TV shows, talk of building a house with cash was a whole other story. It was a commendable ideal, but was it possible? I did my best to stay positive and avoid thinking about the magnitude of what we were attempting. One step at a time, that was all I would allow myself to see. I had even given up on helping Glen to design our house. That was too far ahead. One step at a time. First we needed a foundation. "This is impossible," said Alice. "Only if you believe it is," the Mad Hatter replied. So I believed, and trusted that it would happen, somehow.

Through the hardship that was 2014, this quote by Brad Gast gave me hope. I rediscovered it the summer we moved into the house; it was so fulfilling to see it come to completion:

"No matter what happens, no matter how far you seem to be away from where you want to be, never stop believing that you will make it. Have an unrelenting belief that things will work out, that the long road has a purpose, that the things that you desire may not happen today, but they will happen. Continue to persist and persevere."

We had decided together that this was our path, and it turned out that the decision-making was the easiest part. If it was one thing 2014 taught me, it was tenacity; the ability to hang on, when letting go felt so easy. All I had to do was say enough and it would be done. But the mountain needed to be moved, one stone at a time, as Confucious taught. Perhaps for ourselves, or perhaps, dare I hope, that it might show others it is possible to move the mountain. It is possible, to set the bar high, dream big, forge a new path, and go where no one has gone before, even if only within the history of your family. People can laugh, scoff, doubt, or disregard, but it is still possible, and you can show them.

We came home from camp near the end of August and set to work moving the camper further away from the dig site so it wouldn't hold up construction. That would be the last time it would be moved. We also began cleaning up the dig site of the debri that had fallen in over the last year: mud, rocks, grass growing up. We were scheduled to have a contractor come look at it, and wanted it to be as prepared as possible. Glen's parents had hired my uncle to extend the driveway most of the way up the hill toward our house, and much of that work had been completed, making it easier for cement trucks to get to the foundation site.

We chose a specific contractor because he was connected to our church, and over the phone he gave us a low estimate based on the description we gave. Of course we wanted him to actually come and see it, and we wanted to meet him. That's where the nightmare began.

What followed were several missed appointments, excuses, promises of certain dates to begin work, countless times of nobody answering the phone or returning our calls, and ultimately not showing up to do any work. I was pissed. We had been told this was a great family business to hire, that they were cheap, and did great work, but our relationship ended with me giving them a piece of my mind on their answering machine, since no one ever answered the damn phone.

We lost a whole year. We were banking on that concrete company, because everyone raved about them being such great people. A whole year. "One more winter and we'll be in our house," Glen had said. My ass.

Glen and I started getting grumpy toward each other. He said

I was changing. Said he was afraid we'd end up divorced in ten years. We tried to make the most of the situation and continued remodeling the camper (the one thing we had control over); remodeling the bunk beds and putting down new flooring. Atlas remembers the day we removed the old bunk bed frames to put down the floating floor. The kids slept in sleeping bags on the floor for a couple of days until the new ones were built in their place. I tried washing the 2" mattresses. They were so junky, and probably loaded with invisible mold, but they never felt good enough for me.

One week I gave the bathroom a makeover; repainting the medicine cabinet bright blue, replacing the shower curtain, and after Glen built corner shelves, I purchased a few inexpensive, cute containers to hold bathroom items. That spiced up the bathroom considerably. We also started a fundraiser, using book sales from a Year In a Camper and contributions made through CrowdRise over the next year to build our construction fund. In the end, family, friends, and strangers enlightened by our story donated around $2,300! We were so blessed.

I didn't know that the rift between us was not just stress; that it was the rumblings of childhood trauma coming to the surface at an inconvenient time, needing to be healed, but we took a deep breath and plunged into another unavoidable winter, unsure of what lay ahead.

It's been snowing hard all afternoon and the day is drawing to an end. Glen had a late day at work, as they are in a time crunch to get a certain project done, but he's finally coming home. I can hear the snowblower. He left it at the bottom of the driveway this morning, knowing the snow was coming, and as if to announce his arrival, we can just barely make out the headlight through the snow as he comes up around the corner of the trees. The engine gets louder for a minute, and then quiet again. He'll make a few passes, then he'll get the generator going as the snow covered solar panels haven't been working very hard today (I'll clean those off in the morning). Finally, he'll come inside and strip off his jumpsuit. Supper is almost ready. When he comes in he'll bring an armload of biobricks; compressed bricks of wood shavings that just barely fit in our wood stove, but last a decent amount of time. After supper and chatting with the family, he'll fall asleep on the couch, exhausted. I'll wake him up later so he can get ready for bed, and we'll try not think about the many long, dark, cold days ahead of us. At least there is Christmas. We already have twinkling lights up around the trim of the camper, and our stockings hung from the curtain rod over the couch. A little two foot tree sits on the cover of the water tank. We frequently play Christmas music. It's reassuring and cheerful.

Our fourth Christmas in a camper. I knew we would still be here, but I thought we'd have a foundation; something hopeful to look at. We were distracted from the growing unsettledness by a family trip to Rangley for an extended-family Christmas sleepover party, with a sledding day with my sister, and other fun family activities, but at the end of the day, the depressive spirit would return.

When we moved into the camper, I later told everyone, I had planned on a specific amount of patience to get through. I knew that if it took 2-3 years, I would be fine. Now in early 2015, we were pushing the four year mark, and I had not paced my energy for this. Three years after our record breaking high of 80 degrees on March 22nd, we now were hitting record breaking lows. 10, 12, 8, 14 degrees. It felt like a never-ending winter, figuratively as well as in real life. I wrote in my journal, "is this the life God has chosen for us? Is there a reason for where we are today? Is there something we need to learn from this that we haven't yet? How can we make our current home the dream home that we want?"

Communication continued to be a problem. I expressed unhappiness, he tried to be helpful and put it in perspective. I was frustrated with his business investments, and he was frustrated with the time I invested in projects. I withdrew and quit. I decided this would be the year I closed my doula business, and it was. I sold my gear in February. My ability to be calm, resilient, and hopeful had run out. Looking back on my journals, I realize Glen was also struggling. He was falling asleep as soon as he got home from work, he was frustrated at work, and he was undoubtedly feeling increased pressure as the man of the house to be strong and to provide, despite our trials. We needed immediate evidence that we would not be living in the camper much longer. He agreed to start house hunting with me.

The evenings of late winter and spring were often spent

scrolling through houses on the market. We looked primarily at fixer-uppers and those about to go to auction. Houses we could make a low-ball cash offer on and sign papers right away. House after house, offer after offer, it became more and more clear that God did not intend for this escape option to pan out. Every time we made an offer on a house that had sat unnoticed for months, it sold immediately to someone who could make a higher offer.

One house we went to see with the kids. The price had been dropping steadily for months because no offers had been made. The day we stopped in for an open house tour, a few other families did as well, and even though it needed work, we made an offer, only to learn that for the first time, buyers were scrambling to outbid each other. We couldn't compete.

Back to square one.

Chapter Six

~Love Them Hard~

Spring was in full swing, and this time, we were pulling out all the stops. We called several concrete contractors in June and they all made bids for our job. We chose the company we had the best feeling about, and a month later I fought back tears of joy and disbelief as I watched as the walls of my foundation grow before my eyes.

Hope is a powerful thing. Living hope brings strength to the weary, gives us reason to keep moving forward, even compels us to ignore discouragement, because we know that the thing, we hope for is just on the other side of the next hill, behind the next door, or destined for the next day. Take that hope away, and we find ourselves living on the edge of a precipice. An extreme picture? Maybe. But for a long year, setbacks we faced put me on that edge, and I had to choose daily: Will I hold on? Or will I give in? Giving in felt so easy, all I had to do was cry enough, and it would be over; pack up our bags and leave. To where? Who knew! But in the midst of that was a feeling of dread; if I lose hope, if I glance to the right or left, the gravity of our situation, what we put ourselves through for the sake of hope, will pull me under its torrent and drown me in misery. Hope, in a sense, was the only thing I could hold onto. It was the only way to remember the value of what we were fighting for, and the reasons we would never go back.

At my lowest, at the end of 2014, I gave us a deadline: either we have progress on the house by next summer, or we're moving. I would pack up the kids and move in with family, and I assumed Glen would follow, but I could not stay another year without having more reason to hope that we would indeed have a house to move into at the end of it all.

People have joked about why I hadn't moved out yet, like they don't understand why I would stay, or even, miss the truth that I had just as much to do with this venture as Glen. And that is where the road divides. This adventure was not and never will be a matter of one of us pulling the other along; it is a joint effort, a unified dream. And when hardships hit in full force, we see them as a situation to face together – we have braced for them, weathered them, and come out in one piece. A bit bedraggled perhaps, but one piece.

Almost everyone we've talked to about our experiences has half-jokingly remarked about how we're still together. The image in their minds of six people living in 200 square feet for six years, in difficult conditions, seems to leave them in wonder that we are yet happily married and even close friends. One follower of our late blog, American Family Now, commented about how inspired she was to see a family tackle a daunting project, make it truly a family venture, and above all, we still happen to like each other! Another woman I met in person shared how the attempt to build a self-built home is what ultimately broke her marriage, and so she said she was, for lack of a better word, impressed to see us working so well together.

Marriage, and healthy relationships, is an issue near and dear to our hearts because of broken relationships within our family. I know all too well the preciousness of a loving relationship, so it is from this perspective that I can genuinely say, I know exactly why Glen and I still have a solid relationship.

When a couple is put through a test of strength, when they must travel through murky, unexplored waters, and rely on each other to stay afloat and survive, you witness them at a defining moment in their lives, in which the truth is revealed. Will they be partners; holding each other up through the darkest, most challenging times? Or will the hardship be the ax that drives the awl through the cracks in their relationship, as they struggle to find their own way? And when the test reveals the truth, I believe it also determines the future strength of their marriage. If a couple struggles through their first traumatic experience together, they'll be more likely to continue struggling through the next hardships, whereas a couple who finds a way to use their relationship as a binder of wounds, will create a seal between their hearts, like the gold that the Japanese traditionally use to seal cracks in broken, yet desirable bowls. You find a way to use the situation to make you stronger rather than watching it all die. As the popular song goes: "what doesn't kill you makes you stronger." Glen and I didn't die to each other, because this crazy-ass adventure wasn't our first storm.

Early in our relationship, Glen and I faced hardship that would have split most young couples quickly. For whatever reason that we can only attribute to the grace of God, that experience only tied us closer together. So when Glen was laid off from his high-end carpentry job in 2010, we fast-tracked our plans to homestead, moved our then family of five into a camper in the middle of the woods, and at no point was our marriage pushed to the brink, because we had already been through the fire. Having given up or lost most of my personal belongings in the midst of many moves in my teen years, and having been through traumatic relationships together, I knew that the most important thing in our lives was not a house, money, or other things, it was our people. As long as we had each other, we would be stuck like glue; we could take anything that was thrown at us.

Glen and I have been married for 15 years and together for 20. We're still learning and growing, and we're certainly not experts on relationships, but I would like to think that we have learned enough from our own lives to be able to pass on some ideas of things that have worked for us. All couples with healthy relationships will find their way and figure out what works for them; our toolkit is not for everyone, but there are specific things we have prioritized in our lives that have supported us through stressful times, big projects, life-changing events (good and bad), and personal recovery and growth for us both. When it comes right down to it, if you're going to have an adventure (or survive a major transition even) with your life partner, you have to be on really good terms with them. You have to be on the same page with your goals, be honest about your limitations (be vulnerable together!) and remember that if it isn't serving your relationship, it's not worth it. Your relationship, your family, always comes first. If you have found your tribe, you love them hard: you place them at the top, and all else, no matter how exciting, come next. Why? Because while most things can be adjusted and reevaluated, you can't replace people you love. People are always the most valuable.

Spend time alone to be a couple. If you have kids, or even just a busy lifestyle, it's crucial to carve out time to just be together, the two of you. One of our favorite things is to take walks in the evening. We leave our kids at home and decompress with some physical activity. We also have gotten better over the years at taking date nights, and almost every year we will go somewhere else, childless for a night. And despite being in a tiny home, we also managed to prioritize intimacy. Be together, play together, remember who you were before life carried away with you.

Protect your personal space. In the days when we had four kids ages five and under, I remember getting totally and completely "mommied out." I didn't want anyone to touch me or talk to me. Hell, even look at me in a way that suggested I needed to do something for someone. I needed space. But when you live in a tiny home surrounded by five people, how can you find time or space to be alone? Glen and I both wanted to make sure that we each had personal space, and even the children, as they grew bigger and expressed the need for personal space (our oldest was ten when we moved out). When the buttons were getting pushed, we made it a point to protect each other.

"Mama needs space in the bedroom right now. Leave her alone."

"Nemo is using that space for a project right now, come over here with your toys."

Headphones to block noise became very helpful tools as well. It wasn't ideal, but I think we all learned valuable lessons, the hard way, in understanding the importance of respecting other's needs for personal time and space, and also how to ask for it for ourselves. How does this relate to our marriage? When you have personal space, you feel happier, refreshed, and also far less likely to build resentment against each other. When you are healthier alone, you're healthier together. Or in simpler terms – if I was all touched out from kids, why would I be excited to be together with Glen? And if I'm not excited, then he's frustrated too, and no one is happy. And you know what they say: If Mama ain't happy…

Practice talking. Don't quote me on this, but isn't communication one of the top issues cited in a failed marriage? It's right up there with money. When I have talked to couples about where the arguments happen, a lack of communication or a failure to value the other's opinion and work with it are often brought up. And yet it's so crucial. The funny thing is that it's the same thing we teach our kids when they are young – how to listen, to wait your turn, to be a peacemaker, and here we find ourselves faced with a grownup version of the same conversation. I guess the only thing I would add from personal experience, and not try to add to the plethora of marriage advice, is to talk to your spouse as your best friend. Best friends may still argue, but they share secrets, they have each other's best interests at heart, they stay up way too late talking for the joy of it. That is the kind of communication that we feel has really supported our relationship.

Speak positively about each other. Speaking of communication, when we talk about each other to others, we consider how it would feel to be the one being talked about. I don't complain about my husband to my friends. I will be honest if I need advice or feedback, but I don't whine and complain, and it really bothers me when someone else complains to me about their spouse. If I have a problem with my husband, I talk to him, and I keep my speech about him respectful and in a heart of gratitude, and he does the same for me, which makes us both feel loved.

Help each other. Last but not least, we look for ways to help each other, and we ask for help when we need it. Some of our homestead responsibilities are divvied up based on physical strength, or knowledge, or convenience, but it's not unusual for one of us to just say, "I need you to do this for me today," and we make it happen. There are two pieces to this. One, we don't make assumptions that the other will guess our needs, and two, we almost always answer with a yes. We're a team and we help each other. And when you live off-grid, that teamwork is indispensable.

One of the lowest points in our relationship, while it happened during our camper season, had nothing to do with our living situation, but was a period of time in which I began reliving the aforementioned trauma.

It began, as far as I can tell, in 2014. We were unsettled, trying not to be discouraged about the slow progress on the house, and I had an early miscarriage in the summer. Add it all up and you get an emotional woman reevaluating her purpose and place in the world. Lots of big feelings. It was the perfect conditions for old memories, survival skills, and lies about my identity to surface. The next two years involved lots of processing, tears, panic, stretching, vulnerability, and learning. I had to find my true voice, and separate Glen's identity from the aggressor identification I unnecessarily gave him in my temporary victim mode. The poor man had to be so patient!

It was a rough couple of years and strained our relationship. Living in a small space, having four children in five years, and recently going through a year of unemployment didn't help but having come through the darkness of recovery from PTSD, I feel like a much stronger woman, and we both value our marriage so much more. We have since used this experience to sustain us when Glen had to do some personal growth work related to baggage from his own past, which was aggravated for a while when he got into the bad habit of relying on energy drinks to get through long, stressful days.

Most people have baggage. Few are the people who go through life and escape emotional pain that haunts. It's part of being human. Marriage is an arena where we fight our demons together – or misplace our focus and fight each other instead. This is going to happen regardless of your home's conditions, your finances, your kids' health, or any other thing, but each of those can be straws on the camel's back, and if you don't see the source of the pain for what it is, living off-grid in a camper or being dealt a hard hand will only add to the harshness of the trial. Name the demon, and it takes a direct hit.

In the middle of it all, everything I had been so confident

about before, I now called into question. I wanted to quit anything I started, cancel out obligations, and try to be that idyllic image of a homesteading woman in the hopes I could earn approval as if I didn't have it already. In 2015, I gave up my work as a doula after 12 years of investment into my business, I stopped writing the blog I kept for our homestead adventures after five years of posting and gaining hundreds of followers, and I gave up on a book project in its early stages. I lost all confidence. I thought I would never see shore again, that I would be stuck playing old lies in my head forever.

All of that changed when I received a call from my mom about a job opportunity. The school she is a president of was looking for a part-time teacher for elementary grades, and I was requested personally by the previous president. I approached Glen with it, not feeling confident that I would be a good candidate or that it would be a good move for our family, though it would provide an extra income for the house fund. To my surprise, he encouraged me to do it, and not for the income, but for me – so I could get out of the camper and find a greater purpose. I accepted.

A part-time job became full time within four months, and I stayed there, working mostly with 8-11-year-olds, for three years. It was exactly what I needed. For three years I was able to separate myself for part of the day from the homestead, and it required enough focus that I was unable to worry about my personal problems for significant chunks of time. I had a new purpose: something I could be responsible for. I was needed and valued, and I could master my role. It was no less than life-changing for that season of my life.

2015 was a busy year on the homestead. After our failed attempts to purchase a house in the spring, we knew that building our house was the path meant for us. "Courage, dear heart," C.S. Lewis reminded me. Just keep going. We tried again in June to get a concrete company to come put in our foundation, and suddenly, everything was falling into place. Whereas the year before we struggled in the darkness, now we could see clearly. By the end of July, we had a finished foundation, and had begun ordering materials to cap it off. We met the deadline for my demand the previous fall! Just barely, but exactly when I needed it.

Looking back, I can clearly see the ups and downs of seasonal growth and retreat, joy and depression, often waxing and waning with the seasons. Hindsight looks so different than the present moments, and perspective changes everything, but that summer we were riding a much needed high.

In June, Glen built a screen house and picnic table on a small budget, using quite a few extra materials we had on hand, while Nemo used scrap plywood and 2x4s to construct a tiny clubhouse complete with a hinged door and latch in front of the camper. Our first chicks hatched from our own hens, we hosted our first Labor Day camping event for family, Nemo was recovering from herbal treatment of his Lyme Disease, we were starting at the private school soon, and had spent the summer enjoying camp, strawberry picking, trips to the beach, and a getaway for Glen and I to Bar Harbor. We had a long way to go, but stress levels had dropped for the moment, and our roughed-up hope was glimmering again. We were good with that.

On September 27, 2015 we experienced a Lunar Eclipse. It was the first one the kids would remember, so we got them all excited to get up late in the evening after a nap to watch it happen. However, even after hyping it up, we couldn't manage to wake anyone except Nemo. The other kids just rolled back over and were out. So we bundled Nemo up in a jacket and hat, and together we sat on the small wooden steps outside the camper to stare at the night sky.

When we moved to the land, sitting outside just shy of midnight, surrounded by an empty field and trees to all sides felt overwhelming. It was just so big a space; unknown and unexplored. Now it was home, and we sat there handing the binoculars back and forth, taking photos and pointing at the stars. It was quite a different feeling. It was still big, but we had settled into that space and could appreciate the relationship we had built with the land.

The air grew chilly as the seasons changed, but we fired up the trusty wood stove with more biobricks and filled our days with school field trips, carving pumpkins, and making Halloween costumes. Amelia potty trained herself, and just like that we had outgrown babyhood and had four school-age children.

Many people commit to living in an RV. Most who do are couples who travel. They do it for a year, maybe two, say it was the best thing ever, and then put up a for sale sign on their beloved travel trailer and buy a house to put down roots. Those who do it with kids, for similar reasons to us, rarely last longer than a year. The longest lasting family I have met or found so far after extensive research online is our friends who live next door, ironically. I haven't found anyone online who has lived in an RV as a family, boondocking, for more than three years. It's almost always a means to an end, rather than the goal itself, and no one wants it to have to last longer than necessary, because it's a damn hard lifestyle. It requires your best, and puts you to the test every day. If you aren't in it for the long haul, the demands will reveal that to you in short order. But what about those kids? What's it like for the ones that add that extra layer of complexity to an RV lifestyle?

I joked that our kids would probably grow up and show their disdain for our lifestyle by going into debt to get the largest houses they can. While such choices are still years down the road for them, three out of four have expressed an early opinion: one wants to inherit our small home, one wants to build a mansion, and one wants to build a tiny house on our land. Maybe our choices will have a different impact than I feared.

We chose this lifestyle. Our kids did not. To a degree, I have felt regret that some of the negative aspects of our decisions have created a longer lasting impact than I originally expected, but on the other hand, I think the blessings that the kids have received from this experience are also deeper and longer lasting than I expected. Our parenting philosophy has been intertwined into this story, in which we do everything together as a family, but in which we also want our kids to have the opportunity to develop creativity, problem-solving, communication, and appreciation for life; the good and bad, of which they have had plenty on the homestead and through our RV journey.

Before enrolling the kids at our private school in 2015, they had minimal experience with flushing toilets. Flushes made them nervous. To the point that they would finish their business before coming back out to ask permission to push the lever. The day I heard our neighbor's boy (the family who lives off grid) tell our kids how much he disliked flushing toilets, I laughed so hard!

I am grateful for the experiences that living off grid has given to the kids. They are more connected with reality: with energy, food, resources, and bodily functions, for starters, but adding in experiences like going to school for a few years gave them balance.

To be able to do this with kids, you have to make it your priority. There is no other option. That means you can't try to keep up with the Jones' when it comes to gifts, outings, clothing, etc. at least not while you're on a tight budget so you can pay cash for your house. You have to be creative and find other ways to give love to your kids.

Your life will look different as a family, and you will undoubtedly question your decision at times, finding yourself comparing your life to others, sometimes wishing you could do all they do. But you can't. They aren't living your adventure. And if they tried, they'd have to exchange priorities too. Because we're only human and we can't do it all. You choose your life, define your priorities, set your boundaries, and adjust them if you need to, but make them sacred, or your goals will suck the life out of you. If you make it to the end, it will only be begrudgingly.

While we had no plans to begin construction on the house that fall, we used money generously donated through the fundraiser to order flooring joists, rafters, and framing nails, which we celebrated and carefully stacked on top of the foundation to protect them from the inevitable moisture that soaks the ground from fall through spring, thanks to all the ledge. Now that the foundation was in and we had begun collecting materials, we had to come up with a concrete building plan to give to the code enforcement officer. He had approved the foundation, offering generous appreciation for "what we are trying to do up here," and despite our unusual desires for an off grid home, we did our best to cooperate with the town code to make his job easier and keep us on his good side.

The original plan was for a saltbox-style house with everything on the first floor except for the master bedroom, which would look out to the North and command the view of the valley. It was a 600 square foot plan; three times as big as the home we were accustomed to, but even though we were desperate to move and would have been happy with pretty much any house, both of us had an icky feeling about squishing us all into the design we had created. The intention was to maximize space and use nothing longer than 16' framing so we wouldn't have to special order and thus jack up the price. But there had to be something better. After playing around with numbers, Glen realized we could do a complete second floor for just a couple more thousand dollars. And sold! Our saltbox-style house would become a 16x36 cape house with a one-pitch roof. Half a house, as we all joked. After tweaking the design of the stairs, the code enforcement officer approved our new plan, and Glen went to work on the parts list so we could be ready to purchase materials when we received our tax return come February.

To celebrate the last leg of our journey, we made a second paper chain with the kids. Five years prior we had made one in anticipation of moving to the land, and now we were using it to count down the days until we hoped to be in our house for Thanksgiving 2016.

The next couple of months, heading into our fifth winter in a camper, were hopeful. Our days were filled with school, tree climbing, BB gun practice, holiday crafts, and Christmas gift buying and wrapping. One evening our wild children, then ages 3, 5, 7, and 9, ran outside in the dark, dressed as warriors to scare away the boogeyman. Every time we opened that camper door with its latch opening, we gazed with gratefulness at the foundation our house would soon be sitting on.

By the end of 2015, having had some really good conversations with Glen about my emotional health and trauma healing, I was feeling hopeful and grateful. I was even beginning to dream about how I could find purpose using my knowledge as a home herbalist to fill the gaps left behind when I closed Birth a Miracle Services, American Family Now, and stopped writing. I was expectant of full healing.

Some folks, who had followed our story thus far, expressed

that they were disappointed that we had begun pulling back from sharing our story publicly. We had become accustomed to opinionated, yet inexperienced followers voicing their thoughts, but despite the comments about our "decline in publishing decent videos," we ended the year well. We had a foundation, we were getting better doctors for our kids, we had running vehicles, we were streamlining our projects, and there was hope for the future. YouTube trolls be damned, we had a bright future to look forward to.

And then Christmas ended, and pipes froze, the generator froze, the woodstove kept me up all night, our tiny kitchen was crowded with 5-gallon water jugs, and the panic attacks started. Glen said my face would go ashen and I looked like I had disappeared inside myself. In February I wrote, "Feeling cramped. I can't breathe. 200 square feet has broken me, but I feel I need to be grateful, just keep going. When I lose focus I get clotheslined. My rose-colored glasses got misplaced." But the kids kept smiling and playing, school routines filled the days and card games filled the evenings. When the driveway froze over and the car couldn't make it up the hill, we made the walk both ways, admiring the stars and enjoying the fresh air. Glen started bringing home peanuts in their shells and the kids found a new hobby of shelling them out of a wooden bowl at the table in the evenings.

In late January, my sister and her boyfriend took the kids for the night and we went hot tubbing. We found out the next morning that Amelia had come down with the flu during the night and the two of them had learned real quick how to tag-team the puke routine.

"I'll clean her and you clean the bowl." Why is it that kids have a knack for getting sick the day of special events? She was about six hours behind schedule, so we got our date anyway. God bless the family.

Also in January, we said goodbye to a young hen we had adopted. She had a scissor beak and needed special care. Of course, we named her Scissors. Every few weeks, I would trim her beak with dog toenail clippers and sand it, and every day I would mix her chick food with water, but that sweetheart was worth the effort. Scissors was like a little puppy, and every time we came home she would come running to the car to greet us. She loved being held, and when Glen would tinker on a car, she would stand next to him and watch. We came home from school one day and saw a beautiful red-tailed hawk flying overhead. And Scissors didn't run out to greet us. I knew immediately that something was wrong. So I went searching for her and found her curled up in a ball in the foundation site. It seems we scared off the hawk before he could carry her away. Some days of homesteading just plain suck.

February was really hard, emotionally. Some of my journal entries are rather scary. I probably should have gotten professional help. But God was good to me. A cardinal started hanging out by the camper, and I came to recognize his call. He would sit on the rubber seal under the passenger side window of my Durango and preen himself in front of the side mirror. Every morning. He was beautiful. I looked forward to his visits, and I would giggle over his apparent consciousness of his image. "Must look my best for the ladies!" "Look how handsome I am today!" Silly bird. How fortunate you are to be so free. It wasn't until a few months ago that I learned cardinals represent God's presence, self-assurance, and trust. I felt it, even if I didn't know it at the time.

I stopped helping with the house plans to keep inevitable marital disagreements at bay. I knew I would be happy with our house regardless of who designed it. Instead, I enjoyed watching the kids sit at the table beside their Papa at night, graph paper and rulers in tow, to mimic his exciting work. No matter how light or dark the days, they remained hopeful, and for that, I will always be grateful.

Before Spring arrived, the doors, windows, roofing, framing, and sheathing had all been ordered, the snow was melting quickly, we were collecting water from the thawing dug well, and the kids were back to playing in mud puddles. Despite concerns about the lumber yard getting permission to make a delivery on our country road with their large truck so early in the season, they made it happen on March 12th. "They pulled it off! Oh my goodness I am in disbelief! When Glen comes home from work today he is WORKING ON OUR HOUSE!!!" Indeed, that night the kids took turns bolting down the first piece of the sill, and the next day floor joists were already being put in place. We may have been playing games with the fridge that week; packing food in coolers yet again to reset the fridge so it would work properly, but no matter, because no longer did we have to hope in something unseen: it was sitting before our very eyes! The orders were getting delivered, and very quickly, our yard was transformed into the most gloriously messy construction scene I have ever laid eyes on.

Two days before Spring, I attend my 34th and last birth as a doula for my niece, while Glen was home moving windows and lumber to drier places. It felt like being on a teeter totter, bouncing between abundance and depression. We had a nice stretch of building weather in April and the subflooring and walls went up. The alternating tension and compassion between us continued along with the panic attacks. Little moments of grace and appreciation for what we were accomplishing kept us moving. Shall we pick Grape Leaves, Little Bear, or Blue Lava for the exterior trim color? Grape Leaves it is. Glen and his brother got the walls up, and the kids "helped" push up one gable wall. "Did I do most of the work?" Atlas asked. You can hear Papa's encouraging voice cheering them on in the video of the momentous occasion.

The day the roofing first arrived (more on that later), I snapped a photo of Amelia, standing on the bathroom counter, leaning against the mirror while she brushed her hair. Still tiny enough to stand up there. The little moments. The busyness of the job site also kept us entertained. There was some new story every day. Late April a flatbed delivery truck got stuck on the slippery wet grass in our yard and they had to call the boss to come to pull them out using their big pickup.

April's fresh air was amazing. A blessing in itself. We started leaving the door open and blocking the entrance with 5-gallon jugs to hopefully keep the sociable chickens out. It worked. Most of the time. Buttercup, our pet hen with nine lives, regularly let herself in through the screen door when we had one, and ate scraps of food left by the kids under the table.

By the end of April, the house was framed up and much of the walls were sheathed. Within a couple of weeks, that job was complete with the help of our brothers, and there was subfloor throughout the house and plywood treads on the stairs to the second floor, which would remain there until the pine treads replaced them three years later. The code enforcement officer came to inspect our progress, and upon seeing the tall and narrow shape, he said as gently as he could, "You know, it could conceivably blow over." Glen quickly proceeded to heed his advice and installed twice as many hurricane ties from the foundation to the roof as was required by code. After our history, there was no way he would leave that to chance.

And every day that Glen worked on the house, his little helpers were not far away. Atlas and Amelia set to work building playhouses and kitchens using cut off ends of framing stacked into piles on the second floor, as the walls went up around them. With just one month left of school, warmth filling more of our days, and progress happening on the house, you could feel a surge of happiness rising. We all seemed to have more energy to do our work and celebrate each milestone.

On May 15th, after a passing rain shower, we looked outside to discover, not just the end of a rainbow, but an entire rainbow over the woods behind our house! It was positioned just right so that when we stood in our front yard and looked at the house, there was that perfect rainbow arched over our house as if standing guard. It was beautiful, and it felt like a message of love from God. "I see you! Better days are coming. Hang on."

Projects abounded in May. If you've known me for any length of time, you'll understand that I function best when I have several projects going at the same time or I get bored. At school, I was working on a garden box project with my sister. I was so proud that we came up with the design, bought the materials, delivered them (think Rosie the Riveter), and built them to measurement without any help from a more experienced carpenter! It felt like some of the building knowledge needed at home had rubbed off on me!

Also, that month, before school let out for the summer, I decided to start selling doTERRA essential oils. It would be a part of a bigger vision I had, for a business named Laurel Tree Herbals, and I hoped that it would finance the vision therapy that I so hoped to provide for our eldest daughter so her strabismus could be corrected and she could learn how to see in 3D. I now understand, that while I need to be busy much of the time to feel happy, I was also continuing to search for purpose and meaning. Our then nine-year-old son was pushing hard against me, and my fears about not knowing how to parent a teenager were rising up. Glen saw me struggling and gave me extra hugs. I just wanted to be accepted, and thought maybe if I did just the right things, was successful at just the right projects, then I would be accepted. Such are the lies we tell ourselves in the midst of PTSD.

Four nights after the rainbow, we woke up suddenly to the

sound of the chickens squawking. It wasn't an entirely unusual sound. Fairly regularly, a hen would jump or trip and knock another over, producing squeals of shock until they settled themselves back on the roost in the coop. But the squawking did not stop. Why does it sound like their metal cage is being rattled? Glen grabbed his high-powered flashlight, stood on the steps of the camper, and directed the beam at the chicken tractor. A bear was rattling the cage!

The bear was standing up on its hind legs, front feet on top of the cage, and it was rocking it back and forth to, apparently, shake loose a few chickens. Glen quickly came back in to grab his gun and shot a round off into the woods as it ran off, not to kill, but to scare it away. We haven't seen any bear since, but it made for quite the story!

The last week of May, having marked our five-year anniversary of living on the land, was spent hauling 20-foot rafter beams up the stairwell to the second floor, and cutting the ends to shape. My grandfather, a carpenter himself, came over to give Glen a hand, and together they got much of the rafters screwed into place. The job was finished just before the end of the month. The structural framing was now complete, and though I could not hope to rely on a specific timeline, we were now in our final year of camper living.

Chapter Seven

~ Non Desistas Non Exieris ~

Living off-grid, in a camper for six years, changes you. It changes you in a way that is nearly impossible to describe in words; even when carefully chosen in a way that does it justice. I think that's because, even if you can sense the feeling, it is the actual experience changing you which creates an image in your mind of what it was like. I have a very hard time attempting to create that picture for others without feeling like the words become invalid as soon as they hit the paper. Perhaps adventures are like art in this way.

The first time I felt like someone really understood, was when I read my friend Renee's experience of thru-hiking the Appalachian Trail with her husband and three children. Renee is an amazing storyteller, and her words about her experience were like a big warm hug – finally, someone gets it! She really understands! Thru-hiking the trail is a completely different adventure than living in a camper,

Renee put my feelings into words in a powerful way. Our physical experiences are unique, but our emotional experiences are strikingly similar. She wrote several passages on her blog, which I share throughout this chapter with her permission. Shortly after six months of living on the trail, she wrote:

"The trail broke me, emotionally, mentally, and finally physically. Never before have I felt as broken as I did while hiking the Appalachian Trail… I didn't hike [it] to be broken. I hiked it to be strong. Instead, once the honeymoon period ended, I mostly felt weak and overwhelmed, irritable and out of control… The irony is that I grieve being done… I miss the beauty you experience only when you're 'out there.' I miss identifying as a thru-hiker, even a reluctant and at times ornery and depressed one." (Fimby.net, Off Trail, August 29, 2014)

I cried as I read her story. She put words to my feelings about my own adventure. No one had done that before. We were full time Rvers, boondockers, "the crazy people out in the woods." Looking back on this season, I see so much pain, and yet, like Renee, so much joy wrapped tightly around it. Later Renee wrote:

"Family thru-hiking was a difficult endeavor and, in those moments, (and months) of self-doubt about why we had taken on something so monumental I sought a sliver of reasoning to hold onto, something to justify why we'd willingly put ourselves through these trials, and conscript our kids to come along… If hope is the audacious belief you can fly, then character is the firm footing from which you jump." (Fimby.net, More Than a Fuzzy Feeling, October 9, 2014)

Renee's writing continued to teach on concepts of the uncomfortable balancing act with hope and adversity, dreams and struggle, belief and perseverance, and I soaked up every word because she was deadly accurate, and I was thirsty for confirmation in the midst of my own wilderness.

When I wrote about our adventure on our blog, I constantly walked a fine line between not enough and too much. Do I share what people want to hear about homesteading, or do I share the raw reality? Do I share the lows along with the highs? Or am I not supposed to make people feel uncomfortable? Because that's what will happen if I do share the whole story! Glen was my censor, and pointed out when "the black cloud" had hung over my writing for too long. On occasion, a family member would call me on some detail in my writing that they took issue with, or even to express concern about my emotional health. Most people just weren't ready to hear the truth. Walking that line was a constant struggle.

There is a facade that lies between homesteaders, or other adventurers, and the rest of society. It says, "yes, living off-grid is hard, but it's also glorious." This facade looks like television renditions of Little House on the Prairie; of children being content playing with corn husk dolls; and of the simplicity of living off your own harvests. But then the world shuts the TV off and goes back to modern life and the reality of the watered-down version is entirely missed.

At some point in my blogging season, followers began buying land and campers and emailing us saying that they were moving off grid because of our story. That was my "oh shit" moment, where I began to panic about the seriousness of blogging our adventure. I realized that if I didn't break down that facade, it could have some pretty serious consequences. I knew that if people were going to be inspired by our experience to be brave themselves, I needed to be honest about what it was really like. This life is extremely rewarding, but it is also so damn hard.

This understanding, about the balancing act that many people expect ("show us a little, but not too much") is exactly why the cable networks turned us down. They didn't really want what we had to offer. It didn't look enough like the TV version of Little House on the Prairie. We learned the hard way that when it comes to homesteading, you have two versions: what people see from the comfort of their own on-grid homes, and what those actually living it experience. Without putting boots on the ground, there is no other way of having that experience.

You have the iceberg that everyone sees: the idyllic log home-small family garden-few chickens homestead, but when you find such a homestead, what you don't see is the largest part of the iceberg, hiding under the surface of the dark water: hard work, risk, loss, blood, sweat, tears, late nights, struggles, failures, persistence, action, discipline, courage, doubt, changes, criticism, disappointments, adversity, and sacrifices. While the comfortable, simple, happy version is what looks most appealing at first glance, the irony Renee spoke of is that all that depth and intensity of the iceberg below is where the real magic happens. As the popular quote says: the real magic happens outside of your circle of comfort. It is in the depths of raw hardship that one meets their true self, comes to terms with it, and creates their life around their new vision. Some people say that you can't appreciate the light without sitting in the darkness for a bit, but I say it is in the darkness that one finds the light. You cannot have light without shadow. They are necessarily united.

"We pulled this thing off. There are days, still, when I question the sanity of what we attempted to accomplish, the audacity of it. "[It was] such a paradox. How something so difficult and breaking could also be the positive defining experience in this season of family life. All the times I wanted to crawl into a cave, to retreat, to be rescued, I held onto hope that in finishing, it would all be worth it. And it is." (Fimby.net, The End of Our Journey is Just Our Beginning, November 25, 2014)

Ernest Hemingway wrote, "It is good to have an end to journey toward, but it is the journey that matters, in the end." Living off grid in a tiny home was a means to an end for us. By living this way, we could eliminate most debt and afford (albeit slowly) to build a house. Living in a camper was not the goal by any stretch of the imagination, but it was where we journeyed; physically and emotionally.

When friends of ours decided to adopt our lifestyle and follow a similar path, as we were preparing to move into our house, they kept mentioning how much of an impact our attitudes made on them. But it wasn't the fatigue from the journey that made the greatest impact, because as they were shoving off and setting sail, we were catching sight of land and raising a hallelujah. They caught our joy, our gratefulness, and admired the character development that had been demanded of us, and they wanted it too. They wanted to win the race they set before themselves, even though they knew it would be a journey they were not fully prepared for, just like we hadn't been. As of this writing, these friends have been living in their camper for over three years, and their homestead is coming along wonderfully, but I can hear the hidden story behind their progress – they are in the fire; in the thick of it. Their character is growing, and when they come out on the other side, they will be completely worn out, but they will have a renewed appreciation for the gifts of life that they so desired, and they will have the home of their dreams. They will have won the race. They will have experienced their magical transformation.

Jerry Minchey, author of The Truth About RV Living: The Good, The Bad, and The Ugly, along with quite a few other books on RV living, spoke about the dilemma that some folks have when they move into an RV. He said that many will do so thinking that if they sell their house, quit their job, and change their lifestyle, all their problems will be fixed. While he agreed that their lives would be changed, he confirmed that their problems would still follow them, because a change of residence won't change who you are. At the very least, they would create new, but similar problems, because they haven't dealt with the root problem of why those problems happened in the first place. For the most part, I agree with Mr. Minchey. If you sign up for the wrong reasons, you will find yourself blindsided by reality and unwilling to change in order to fix their problems, but there are those who know they are signing themselves up for a "school of life," and are prepared to learn the lessons. These are the strong-willed, yet open-hearted soldiers who carry on and reach the end. When they do, they find they have been changed after all.

I am not the same person I was when we moved here. I have learned the nature of value, priority, importance, hard work, sacrifice, and truth. My character actually has changed, just as Renee's did, and my friends will also. Looking back on this story from the other end, I can tell you that despite the brokenness that happened, it was totally worth it. I found hope in the darkness, joy in the hardship, gratefulness in the lack, simplicity in the work, and perseverance. All the things that are so easy to wish for, but so difficult to work for.

Maybe it's just the birth doula in me, but it seems that so many things in life can be compared to giving birth. Other relatable analogies include parenthood (like I mentioned at the beginning of this story), building a business, going to college, or building a house.

For me, birth looked something like this:

Stage One: "I got this!"

Stage Two: "Oh, shit."

Stage Three: "Just get it done."

Stage Four: "I just want to sleep!"

Stage Five: "I friggin' quit!"

Stage Six: "Wait, it's done?!"

There is also a seventh, "postpartum" stage, of processing all that has happened, understanding it, reckoning with it, and deciding what it means in relation to moving forward. Where do I go from here? This is found in the months or years after giving birth, where you see moms sharing their stories with each other over and over.

Ironically, the way I processed our journey of moving into a camper, living off-grid, saving up for and of building our house, followed this process to the letter, with each stage lasting roughly a year. It took six years and two months to get into our house ("wait, it's done?!"), and as I write this nearly three years post-move, still living in an unfinished house (because, time and money), I can see that my processing has been finished. I can look back on our journey, as Renee did on her own, and see that even though I always wanted to retreat and to be rescued at times, we did cling on to hope, and we did make it, and it WAS all worth it in the end.

When the frame of that house went up, it was like a rallying cry had been let loose, loud and clear. We heard the hard and fast drum rhythm in our hearts. It was time to push that baby out. We were almost home. We stopped waiting for the proverbial light at the end of the tunnel, and as the popular quote says, "we lit that bitch up ourselves." It was time to kick some ass.

By the beginning of June 2016, the framing was complete. Next came sheathing, wall studs, ice and water shield, and roofing;

each piece of metal carefully clamped and hauled up by a rope to the top of the house to be screwed in (but not before we got a picture of all the kids on the roof!). The porch roof went up, followed by drip edge and trim. We finally decided on a layout for the bathroom and got that framed out along with the rest of the rooms.

At night, after putting the kids to bed, we would take walks or escape to the screen house for some quiet, and work by the light of a lamp on our personal projects, stopping now and then to listen to the sounds of critters in the woods, and mull over the significance and emotion of this new season.

The progress came quickly, but setbacks just as much so. In early June, Glen had to pause the construction work so he could bleach all the plywood and lumber which were growing mold. It had been exposed to the elements long enough that it had started to become damaged, and it certainly didn't help that we had so much rain that spring that there was a standing puddle in various places on our new floor. Then a wind storm came up seemingly out of nowhere and ripped up a huge section of ice and water shield laid out on the roof. That was incredibly frustrating, but the cost of the damage was thankfully less than expected.

A couple of weeks later, we discovered that one of the windows, still new in its package and leaning against a wall in the house, had a nice big crack extending out of a little pit that looked like a BB would fit in perfectly. No one fessed up, but we brought the window to the local glass shop and had it taken care of within a couple of weeks.

Despite the excitement of building our house, life continued to keep us busy elsewhere. It's impossible to set all else aside to focus on one thing completely. Early summer also brought many blessings. A friend of a friend gifted us with a beautiful four-poster bed, a bookcase, and a hutch. I had dreamed of a four-poster bed my whole life. God saw my desire and blessed me with a home and a free, four-poster bed. We shared fun moments with family, roasting marshmallows, having water balloon fights, and celebrating our kids' 4th, 6th, 8th, and 10th birthdays with 30 kids for 3 hours in a camping-themed birthday party.

Early in the summer, with help from a friend's farm, our broody hen, whose eggs stopped developing, was able to adopt four little chicks. She took to them immediately and devoted the next several weeks to their care, in a large dog crate outside our door, until she felt they were big enough to be left while she rejoined the other hens. The kids each named one of the chicks. They were called Sauron, Cocoa, Margaret, and Nova, and it gave us great pleasure to watch their mother, Mustard, take them for walks around the edge of the field to look for food. One day I caught her breaking up a squabble between the boys, who immediately started fighting when she turned her back. I could relate to that poor mother hen, and I laughed.

My boys build a zip line with the help of a couple of friends, out of a rope strung between two trees. It provided hours upon hours of fun. Forts in the woods were built up over the course of the summer with scrap wood, cloth, and rope. Many paper airplanes were thrown from the second floor of our new house.

A canceled getaway thanks to hand, foot, and mouth disease for Independence Day weekend gave us extra time to sand and paint window trim. Nemo tried his hand at it too. Hours and hours of painting trim green followed. I was thankful when I could work with a new color!

We did get to watch the fireworks and eat ice cream just before I succumbed to the illness as well, which slowed me down for a frustrating few days, but the endless trips to Home Depot continued, and the porch roof went up. By the end of the month, Glen had also found time to build a hot tub; a beautifully paneled and trimmed out IBC tote by the screen house. The kids nicknamed it the cold tub because Glen's attempts at heating it with solar via black tubing and a pump were less than effective, but it was enjoyed regularly at the end of hot workdays nonetheless.

Nemo had his first experience indoor rock climbing with his great aunt, we visited a local bird sanctuary, went swimming at a friend's house on the lake, visited Range Pond State Park, and finally, we got our two-night getaway.

In August, we took the kids to Enchanted Forest Day at a nearby wildlife park for Daphney's 8th birthday, and for the next month, she and Atlas were building fairy huts with twigs, pine needles, pretty rocks, and little odd toys from their collections. We also went miniature golfing for the first time as a family, and spent a lot of time at school, working on my classroom and rebuilding their playground with a new giant swing set, a sandbox, a jungle gym, a cabin, and fencing. It was finished the day before school started!

At night, we frequently held stakeouts for raccoons; those cute little buggers were the bane of our flock of chickens. One night we caught four of them on video, eating out of the chicken food kept in the makeshift woodshed. They noticed us and went back to eating. Didn't matter how many times we caught and disposed of their friends – they would show no fear.

Telling the story of how our house was built would not be complete without a telling of the roof saga, in which we learned that you cannot ever order roofing from Lowe's without expecting some kind of drama. It is a mess of a story, that lasted upwards of three months, and I conscripted Glen to help me remember how it went down, but I think we got it.

It all started when the 13 roofing sheets we needed first arrived in the spring along with our other building materials. Some we ordered from Lowe's, and some from a local lumberyard, who has always been great to work with. Now, because of a prior order with Lowe's, Glen anticipated that while customary, there were no extra protective sheets added to the top and bottom of the roofing stack, so when the wind bent one panel in half, he assumed that a replacement needed ordering.

Phase two of the roofing saga commenced. A single sheet of replacement, acrylic-coated, galvanized roofing was ordered. No big deal. But when Glen borrowed a trailer to go pick it up, he realized it was bent down the middle. Because communication is predictably difficult between employees there, Glen recorded a video of them confirming that they would replace the bent piece and deliver it free of charge.

Phase three. Lowe's calls to say the roofing is ready to be picked up. They had no record of a delivery slip but finally agreed to deliver it when Glen mentioned the video. The third time is supposed to be the charm, right?

They delivered a bent piece.

On to phase four. Again, a fight for delivery. Turns out they don't even have a system for recording payment for delivery of special orders. When Glen realized that the delivered roofing was a different color than the roofing we already had, the delivery guy apologized and expressed embarrassment for our sake.

Five. Lowe's called to inform us that our roofing was ready for pickup. Glen followed up his now predictable rant about delivery with a question: "Is this piece acrylic-coated galvanized metal?" After a pause, the employee responded, "we have a problem."

Ultimately, it turned out that the original sales rep asked us if we wanted our galvanized roofing acrylic-coated. We paid the extra fee, but we were not informed that acrylic coating was not an option for galvanized roofing. The sales rep had made a false claim, which we paid for, and then we were shipped plain galvanized. The replacement galvalume was put back on the shelf and Lowe's called (phase six) to tell us our roofing was ready to be picked up: the plain galvanized to match our original order. After going through the story yet again with yet another rep, they complained that they can't safely deliver one piece, so Glen coached them over the phone on how to brace it with 2x4s. It was delivered in one piece. The right color. Thank God.

Ironically, it was later discovered that the original shipment did indeed come with a protective sheet, so Glen and his brother had enough to do the job all along... until they accidentally dropped a piece off the roof, and the replacement piece was needed after all. Moral of the story: be careful who you order your roofing from, and be ready to advocate for yourself.

The next big push on the house came Labor Day weekend in September. My family came for our annual camp-out in the yard, and the men came with their work pants and willing hands. I sat in front of the house, in silence, my heart full of happiness and gratitude, as I watched them climb all over the staging, in and out of holes in the plywood intended for windows, shouting bits of helpful information to each other in anticipation of what they were about to do. The house wrap went up, and I sat in awe as the first window went in. And then another. And another. And then the pre-assembled trim we had been working on for weeks, and then the front door. And I couldn't believe it. The structure we had invested so much in suddenly took on the look of a house, and my heart swelled with joy. We couldn't move in yet, but I could see the shoreline up ahead and I was ready to start kissing that beach!

All I could think about was how big those gorgeous windows were, and how I was going to open and close them, without gears and keys stripping out, and how heavy those beautiful screens were that wouldn't easily pop out of their frames. These were REAL windows. They were OUR windows, that WE chose and installed. And that door. With a real doorknob and real windows, and it would open and shut like a normal door (to borrow an expression from our eldest son). The whole experience was rather surreal. The shell of our house, five years after digging our foundation site, was taking shape and becoming our home.

The campers left, but the work continued. Glen used the dining room table in the camper to paint pieces of trim Royal Purple for the doors, and all the trim that tired me of painting Hunter Green over the summer was hung up around the remaining windows. All this momentum inspired me to do a major overhaul of cleaning in the camper, and I minimized our belongings again to keep the things I really felt like moving into our house. Once the basic structural needs were done and the house was closed in, our work on the house drew to a standstill for the winter. Looking out the tiny camper windows at the house sitting before us gave us renewed hope. We would arrive at the end of the journey after all.

The kids went back to school. This year in Kindergarten, 1st,,3rd, and 4th grades. The emotions of watching the kids grow up and no longer share a classroom; of me no longer teaching my two babies, was intense some days, but it was healthy growth and school kept us busy as we passed the time. That winter could not pass quickly enough.

American Family Now was officially closed, but our stories of camper living and construction continued on social media. After continuing to struggle with feeling like a burden all summer, I was feeling less sad and more confident with my choices. I started creating a vision for my dream of an herbal company. We were still in a rough season with our marriage; me feeling like I was not meeting his expectations and he being a rather unhappy person to live with, but we had still made large strides together over the previous year, and both of us expressed the desire to continue working on ourselves to better our relationship.

October brought electrical work along with the Fryberg Fair, Nemo's first hunting trip, an egg-bound hen fiasco, date nights, and trick-or-treating on Halloween. Connecting wires and boxes didn't feel as momentous as window installation, but progress was progress, and we spent chilly evenings under the light of a utility lamp, conversing after the kids went to bed, as Glen moved from one room to the next, and asked me for my thoughts on where outlets should be placed.

In November, we hunted one Saturday morning for the perfect Christmas tree on our land, finally settling on a semi full-limbed pine tree. We set it up in the house, where the dining room table would sit less than a year later, and decorated it with all the ornaments we hadn't been able to use for seven years. Christmas music played on a Bluetooth speaker in the background, and Glen hung the stockings, handmade by my late great aunt, from nails in our bedroom door frame. It was the most beautiful thing; a bit of Christmas in the middle of a construction site, and we admired it while bundled in our winter coats, hats, and gloves.

Before the snow arrived in November, we had family photos taken. My favorite was of the six of us all jumping in the air at the same time, the view of the surrounding mountains in the background. Our photographer also snapped a photo of us sitting on the front stairs of the house. A snapshot of who we were as our house was built up around us.

Meanwhile, Atlas needed trips to the chiropractor for knee and hip injuries sustained from a fall at the playground, we had cousins over for the night, Nemo's Lego was set up on the table in the camper as he began exploring stop motion videography, and our favorite hen disappeared for several days.

Once the snow started falling, it meant business. Shortly after our first, glorious Christmas morning opening presents in our cold house, a blizzard dumped so much snow it came up to Glen's hips. It took him two hours to snow blow a single path the 700 feet to the road and to unbury the cars and the solar panels. As the kids came in from their play in the wintry wonder landscape (imagine a giant field of undisturbed white gold), I carefully piled their wet boots, gloves, and hats on the top of the radiant kerosene heater in the hopes they would dry out a bit before the kids headed out once again. Jackets were hung on coat hooks above the door, so you literally had to push them aside to walk into the camper. In a silly mood one day, surveying the mess of winter gear dumped all over the entryway, I posted on Facebook: "We are now entering the time of year when, due to all the gear hanging up or piled up in the camper, it feels like walking through the wondrous land of Ward Robe, in the country of

Spare Oom to get outside." The day after that blizzard, we stayed up until midnight at my mom and stepdad's to welcome in the New Year – the year we would move into our house.

Before settling into our winter routine, I wrote on Facebook:

"I had a moment tonight, one of those when you're like, 'oh shit, what did I just do?!' Let me tell you friends, this is one hard journey to be on, and I am so incredibly anxious for it to be over!! I keep putting off thinking about the trials of winter in a camper, just taking it one day at a time, but somehow it just seemed overwhelming tonight. How am I doing this again?! For the 6th time?! Oh, all the complaints I could spew from my mouth right now! And yet, there is so much good as well, so many blessings I can recount. I know there is a good reason for all of this, and I will be so much more grateful for the result than I ever would have been for it in the past. Not just excited, but like, let me kiss the floor of this house like I just landed after a sickening voyage over stormy seas kind of grateful. I can't even put into words how anxious we ALL are at this moment in time. Holding our breathe. Counting down the days. Can this winter please just be over already?! But spring will come. I know it will. It always does. It has to."

There was so much snow. On days when school was closed, which were far too many in number, the Lego came out and covered the camper, which entertained for a while, but we were all anxious to get back to school each time. Glen would play his new compact electric guitar and I could be found folding laundry at the table or hiding out in my room with my journal or a good book. During vacations, I would work on cleaning the kids' room, again, or sorting through their artwork, again. Their room got messy so fast. They would dump all their toys in the center of the narrow floor space and pile up blankets and pillows in the doorway to create some kind of blockaded fort. It looked like a tornado had passed through.

One snowy day, Glen had the idea to pull out a bunch of random junk from his collection of odds and ends. Metal pieces, dowels, random electronics, fasteners… He helped the kids to build steampunk model guns out of this mixture, from pieces of bent pipe, odd screws, wires, and knobs. They created unique pieces that garnered praise from housebound Facebook friends.

While the hope of an end in sight spurred us on each day, the work required to live off grid never ended. The batteries had trouble keeping up with our draw of power, and the solar panels were frequently covered in snow. One day I woke up to discover the batteries had been buried in thick ice, so I couldn't reset the inverter. I was so pissed, not just about the batteries, but about the whole situation (how things like this kept me too busy to do things I actually wanted to do), that I put a little too much oomph behind the shovel as I slammed it into the ice to break it up, accidentally hitting the corner of the battery. The handle of the shovel bounced back and hit me so hard in the jaw that I could feel myself blacking out. I fell onto my butt, and just before succumbing to the attraction of falling asleep, the passing thought of, "that's not good," kept me from letting go, and I focused on staying awake, sitting there in the snow until I had recovered enough to get myself back inside. I can't remember what I did about the batteries after that. Probably nothing. I only remember sitting on the couch all afternoon. It was another day before I could put enough words together to carry on a normal conversation with anyone. Tantrums don't generally pay off, no matter how well deserved they are.

The driveway continued to pose difficulties. Though it was now covered in gravel, it seemed at times to simply provide a convenient place for ice to build up. It was not unexpected when someone would get stuck on the side of the driveway, having slid off the side into the snow. This wasn't generally a problem if I had my Durango, but if Glen had taken it to work, or if I was the one that slid off to the side, then a call for help was made. One Sunday, on our way to church, which we had recently started doing again, we saw a bald eagle as we left the driveway, and as we all gazed up to admire its beauty, including the driver, we hit a slick patch and wound up spinning the vehicle in the one lane driveway, stuck facing the wrong direction. Some shavings, dirt, shovels, and muscle got us out, albeit a little late.

That icy driveway made for great sliding though, and after sliding right around the corner toward the road, sleds were ditched many times to save butts. "Abandon ship!" was the chosen method of staying safe while driveway sliding.

As long as the snow wasn't too deep, the chickens would still come out to play most days. You could see the trail they made from the chicken coop to camper and woodshed, and rarely would a brave chicken dare to escape the area they prescribed for themselves. One of my favorite chicken moments captured on photo is of Nemo holding a rooster under each arm at the door: Chrome and Falcon; father and son. He always had a way with chickens, even the grumpy ones like Falcon.

On those long days, I also began dreaming of homeschooling again, which I decided on shortly after the school year began. Being at school had been a well-timed gift from God, but we needed freedom again. We would be moving into our house, the extra money wouldn't be as crucial, and being at home would mean I could more easily attempt to meet some needs the kids had. It felt scary, thinking about leaving the guaranteed income, but it also meant increased time and energy to devote to the new business I had officially started with a friend, Laurel Tree Wellness.

February was the hardest month. Mold and wood smoke was rough on Atlas' asthma, and Amelia's arrhythmia was getting worse. I was beginning to panic about the safety of our home environment. I needed out. Thankfully, a trip to the pediatric cardiologist reassured us that her abnormal heart rate was harmless and likely to be outgrown, but I was still worried.

Snow day after snow day kept us cooped up inside.

Sibling. Rivalry. Hell.

Ain't nobody had nothin' on me. In a spare moment, I reposted a meme that said, "when I find that damn groundhog I'm going to kick his ass," to look up and realize Daphney was aiming a slingshot loaded with a Barbie doll head at my face. One particular snow day, when Glen was also stuck inside, the TV started growing streaks of various colors across the screen. Even the TV was saying, "screw you." Another aptly timed meme reminded us, "this too shall pass. It might pass like a kidney stone, but it will pass." Man, that felt like one giant ass kidney stone.

On my gratitude list: It was 80 degrees inside. We could still find the barrel with toilet shavings despite being buried up to the cover in snow. We had at least five water totes lined up by the stove at any given time (surrounded by a towel to soak up melted condensation). Plans for the house continued. Seven-year-old Atlas was often busy cutting down trees with his new hatchet, and he assembled an old computer his uncle gave him as a project. We went swimming at an indoor pool together in March, and the first thaw allowed us to refill our water storage now in the basement of the house. I finally discovered the miracle of listening to music on headphones to block out the never-ending sibling rivalry and general chaos (mothers, do yourself a favor and get yourself a set of headphones). We made our first purchase with our 2016 tax return: stove pipe. We were going to have a real wood stove!

When it comes to living off-grid, I feel there are a number of things we boondockers come to appreciate in fullness that appears way too simple when it comes to the discussion with "outsiders." When a woman used to creature comforts offhandedly told our RV-friends she would "love to live that way," my friend's internal response was, "you have no freaking clue." There are joy and satisfaction in living "this way," but when you say, "we use solar power," or "we have a compost toilet," it's just way too simple and incomplete. Try this one on for size: "every couple of days, Glen has to carry outside the five gallon pail that we shit in." That sounds a lot more visceral, doesn't it? It's not bad, it's not good. You assign the implication behind that statement, but at least now we're getting a genuine picture without the pretty wrapping of "compost toilet."

Or let's look at solar power for example. We decided to save money by not buying a kit, but by piecemealing the supplies we would need to rely on solar power. It absolutely saved us money, and it works well for us, but it's not the prettiest setup like you see images of online. Our solar panels are literally leaning on the back wall of our house where they will get the most sunlight. Wires attach through a basement vent to the charge controller, batteries, and inverter before it goes up through the wall to the power box hidden behind a picture on our bedroom wall. When the batteries are working properly, we will go long periods of time without needing the generator (unless we're running power tools) during the summer, but because we live in dark, cloudy Maine, we generally need the extra power it can provide for a few hours a day in the winter. With this power, we run lights, charge electronics, run a small TV and small kitchen appliances, as well as running the pump that pushes water from the storage barrels in the girls' closet to the shower and sinks, and another pump to push water from the storage outside, upstairs. We recently made the transition from a gas fridge to an electric fridge with an energy-efficient compressor, and from a gas stove to a hybrid stove running mostly on propane. To accommodate the extra power draw, we purchased an extra four solar panels and will put two more batteries into circulation, but we still need to run the generator when we bake anything because the heating elements require a large amount of electricity. Microwaves are out of the question, and we can only vacuum midday or with the generator.

Running solar is not fail-proof. When it's dead of winter and the generator is literally frozen, we are up the you-know-what creek. But on the other hand, when the power goes out on the grid around us (which it does, several times a year), we wouldn't even know if we didn't have family local to us. There is a meme that floats around occasionally of a group of Amish men chuckling, and it says, "oh, you're out of power? That's too bad." The plus side is, that even though creating your own power is not as easy as flipping a switch, we don't have to deal with evil Central Maine Power, who everyone complains about, and we are sitting nice and comfy when the neighborhood power goes out.

Every off-grid homestead looks different, but ours doesn't include a dishwasher because of the amount of water consumption required. On my grumpy days, I am jealous of everyone's dishwashers and frustrated when they wishfully say, "if only we washed dishes like they used to; by hand!" As if it was all sunshine and roses. 30-60 minutes a day, baby! Yet, I am also grateful that we live the way we do. Not having a dishwasher means either I get quiet time with my headphones on to think, or I have quality time with my husband as he dries the dishes I wash. Nothing can replace that. Science has also shown that microwave ovens, however convenient they are, are actually quite dangerous for long-term health. My oldest has remained largely microwave-free for over two-thirds of his life, and my youngest has never lived with one. With all the potential environmental toxins we are exposed to, that gives me great peace as their mother. When a friend decided to forgo her microwave, she asked me for advice on how to do it. Would it be more convenient than my stovetop some days? Sure. But I am grateful that we don't have one. That is a more complete picture of what it actually looks like.

April provided us with a rush of energy for the final push. Now that spring had arrived, we could pick up where left off on the house again, but this push would be different than the others. This would be the one that brought us home. And once we began, we knew we wouldn't stop until we walked across the threshold of our home for the first time.

The same weekend our friends moved into their camper, our kids had a sleepover, and Glen and I slept on the air mattress in our new bedroom. It was a cool April night to be sleeping in an un-insulated house, but that wasn't going to stop us. The next night, we rolled out sleeping bags in what would be the girls' room, and we all slept in the house. Bacon and eggs were served on the camp stove the following morning. Though it was just for the fun of it and we hadn't moved in yet, it felt like the end and the beginning. The end of our home in the camper, and the beginning of our home in the house. Our hearts had moved.

Five-year-old Amelia was the only one of us who had never lived in a house before. Sadness. Joy. Mourning. Celebration. She was about to embark on a grand adventure. And I was so happy for her and our other three children. It was time.

Mud season had arrived, and Monday through Thursday we walked down the driveway that had succumbed to the pull of nature, to the car parked by the road to get to school. On weekends, the kids worked alongside us as we lugged 2x4s from the trailer to the house. They built structures with scrap wood while Glen hung drywall and I mudded and sanded. The kids stripped down to their shorts and played in the water running down over the ledge and around our foundation, and built streams with mud while we attempted to expand our water storage with a blowup pool. We ordered staging and Glen designed and built a set of steps from iron rods for the front porch. The kids made monkey bars out of the staging, and we filled the minivan on countless trips with 16-foot lumber and boxes of screws. In late April, my grandfather arrived ready to work, and the two men got a good head start on the siding on the front of the house. My grandmother wrote, "the excitement you have is catching. There is so much more to be done, but we can have more hope now that you'll NOT be spending another winter in the camper. Rather your home will be placed within your house. Joy!"

The extra shower curtain rod holding up jackets all winter over the tub finally caved under the weight, and I took the message and packed up the winter gear. Winter was over. Hallelujah!

On the last day of April, as we were about to mark our six-year anniversary of moving to the land, we cooked and ate our first dinner on the camp stove in the house: burgers made on a camp stove. Those were the best damn burgers we'd ever had.

This last winter was hard, physically, but it was also an opportunity for an emotional breakthrough and tremendous emotional growth. At the end of February, I wrote in my journal: "I am standing precariously on a cliff edge. Standing between hating myself and wanting to set myself free." Glen was afraid I would leave. We would alternate between times of peace and times of turmoil in our relationship. I was depressed, anxious, we were sick a lot, I wasn't sleeping, people were canceling their commitments with me, and I was overwhelmed at work. I would end up having another miscarriage on Mother's Day weekend, and one of my best friends started disconnecting herself from me, eventually leaving entirely. I felt drawn to wild women. I needed strength. I felt I must have distanced myself from God, but looking back I can see he was a priority all along – an unchanging staff I could lean on. It is in these dark moments that breakthroughs seem most likely to happen. That winter had been the hardest of all in some ways, but it was also the beginning of a new season. A difficult birthing of something glorious. Our marriage, and my emotional health, is in the wonderful place it is today because through the work we accomplished together in building our home, we faced our demons. Demons in our marriage. Demons in my past. And also the demons that came with choosing a strange lifestyle, of paving a new way.

I would look around at other families, having money and time to do normal family things, and I longed for this journey to be over so we could do those things too. My unrealistic fears led to images of the kids being grown and out of the house, having not experienced normal childhood adventures to the ocean, to the movies, to Santa's Village, or whatever, because we had to be stingy to finish the house. The reality is, they were also gaining adventures and experiences many kids don't have, like helping to build their own house, building forts in the woods, and barrel riding down the hill. Comparison is a hard voice to listen to, but even more difficult to ignore. Especially when the path you choose is hard for most to accept. "If you don't sacrifice for what you want, what you want will be the sacrifice." So what did we want?

A home. A recession-proof home no bank could take from us. A home we could pay for once and for all with one income and no interest. A home we didn't have to be on the grid in order to manage. A home we could give to our kids if they wanted it someday. It was an investment in their future; in our future. The sacrifices sucked, but we never wanted to be in a position again where what we wanted was forced into sacrifice. Even from the beginning, we knew there was a possibility that we might not reach our goal, but we also knew we couldn't give up when our vision was everything we wanted. Nothing worth having is easy to get, and the only way to get it was to keep going.

Sacrifice was a lesson I worked through that winter, but so was fear. Fear about safety, about health, about finishing, about hardship in general. We had decided not to fear the unknown of this journey, and each time frustrations abounded, we had to recenter ourselves and remember hope; to remind ourselves of our goal, our priorities, our why. Hope was a living word, as our pastor reminded us. It is not wishful thinking; it is trusting God with the outcome – an active decision to release fear. The fear and frustration still felt so intense, but we couldn't act on it, to the best of our ability. God isn't a god of fear, but of faith, hope, and love. "Fear not" is the most recited command in the Bible. In all aspects of our lives, He wants us to have the peace that comes with acting courageously in hope. Because He's already got the outcome and the way there figured out.

This is the story I wanted to share. No adventure is without hardship. No unbeaten path can be trekked without worn out shoes and branches thwacked in the face once in a while, but if we never leave the safety and predictability of home, how else will we ever see the views at the top of the mountain, or capture creatures through the lens, or experience the thrill that comes from pushing ourselves passed our preconceived comfort zones?

It is said that life begins outside your comfort zone, and I do believe this. The thrill is for real! But the inseparable colors, of bright and dark tones, are so much deeper, so much richer and more meaningful, when the real feelings smash through the figurative and real screen that is an attempt at self-preservation. It makes the story truer. And the doubt expressed by a few commentators on our story has been far outweighed by letters of gratefulness from people who found inspiration and encouragement from our story of triumph.

They are the ones I keep writing for.

For as Theodore Roosevelt so wisely proclaimed: "It is not the critic who counts; not the man who points out how the strong man stumbled, or where the doer of deeds could have done better. The credit belongs to the man who is actually in the arena; whose face is marred by dust and sweat and blood; who strives valiantly; who errs and comes short again and again; who knows the great enthusiasms, the great devotions, and spends himself in a worthy cause; who at the best knows in the end the triumph of high achievement; and who at the worst, if he fails, at least he fails while daring greatly; so that his place shall never be with those cold and timid souls who know neither victory nor defeat." Or as Brene Brown succinctly put it, "if you aren't in the arena also getting your ass kicked, I'm not interested in your feedback." Whatever your adventure, as with our own, it's time for truth; for breathtaking highs and depressing lows to be joined together to create the whole, beautiful picture.

Never give up, never surrender, and for God's sake, keep it real!

Chapter Eight

~We Got This~

What keeps you going when every part of your mind and body is screaming at you, "for the love of God, please stop!" When you are exhausted from lack of sleep, overwhelmed by your temporary home falling apart, your muscles are throbbing, your nerves are going numb, you're breathing heavily through a dust mask, and you're frustrated at not being available for your kids while you work so damn hard for them?

At different stages of this journey, this plea varied in its wording, but its common theme has pulled us forward on the marathon set before us to keep going, keep moving forward, don't stop, keep your eyes on the goal. But the end goal was always so far away, just out of reach, that we had to continuously hold on to the hope that every movement, every effort, every exertion made a difference and pushed us closer to what we desired so heavily: a home. A home for our children, a home to grow old in, a home to love people in, a home no one could take from us. So when our bodies hurt, and our hearts were frustrated, and we just wanted to throw in the towel, this pulled us forward and compelled us to keep pushing past the wall we never knew for sure if we could overcome – this home.

"Sometimes the strength within you is not a fiery flame that all can see, it is a tiny spark that whispers softly, 'you got this, keep going." ~
Deepak Chopra

Those three months of April, May, and June 2017 were the most intense and demanding out of the whole journey. It was the pushing of our greatest creation out into the world, in which our entire beings were required to focus our energy and to eat, sleep, and breathe this birthing process of building our home. If there was one word that summed up that spring, it would be endurance. When the going got tough, and I didn't want to go on anymore, like a birthing woman I repeated my mantra. Only instead of my usual, "come on, baby!" it was "we're going to have a house," over and over and over. We're going to have a house. The pace we kept only ramped up in June after the school year ended. We had set a moving date of July 7th, and come hell or high water, the house was going to be ready for us!

In order to feel comfortable moving in, we wanted the kids' rooms to be completely done, with the exception of the floor, so that we wouldn't have to keep moving their stuff to finish walls once they moved in. We also wanted the drywall on all the walls, even if it wasn't completely mudded, sanded, and painted. The kitchen, bathroom, and living area wouldn't be anywhere close to being done, but that was okay. We could still use the camper's resources until the pipes froze later in the year. Even still, there was a lot of work to be done before July 7th.

The code enforcement officer paid us a visit early in the spring after the electrical had been done. He needed to see the framing before we closed in the walls. He gave us the go-ahead, only disapproving of the iron stairs on the front porch because it didn't give a three-foot landing outside the door, but that could be remedied. As of this writing, he still needs to see the front and back porches, as well as the plumbing and propane hookups before we can officially have our complete approval. Glen will have personally handled every single piece of the house, except for the pouring of the foundation, and a lot of the mud and taping. Every piece of wood, drywall, screw, nail, metal… all of it.

On a single day in May, Glen moved 136 full sheets of drywall up the stairs into the house, and some of it up the second flight of stairs. As a result, he developed bursitis in one shoulder, and damaged nerves in his elbow that would send shooting pains through his arm if he moved the wrong way.

After waiting to do a lot of the drywall and painting until school let out for the summer, I started pulling several hour shifts at a time, sometimes more than once a day. The repeated and heavy use of my wrists caused me to develop a ganglial cyst the size of a quarter and ulnar tunnel syndrome in one wrist. But we kept going. My wrists would heal over time, but Glen never fully recovered.

There was an interesting play between family life and working on the house. Just because our attention was highly absorbed by the project, it didn't mean our lives stopped. Our children were a blessing in this sense; they reminded us to stop and look around once in a while. One afternoon I would be taking the kids for a nature walk down the dirt road, and after his work that evening, Glen would be building the light fixtures for the house. One Saturday, our work was interrupted by a cry for help. Amelia had gotten herself stuck 20' up a tree and couldn't get down! We normally let our kids push their limits, but she was banned from climbing for a while. The kids found the most ingenious ways of getting attention when we were working!

Glen made the light to go over the dining room table by soldering four light bulb fixtures to a wheel from an old cart found out back of the wood manufacturing plant where he worked. He attached an iron rod he bent into a "U" shape, from which it would hang from the ceiling on a length of chain and painted it all black. The kitchen light he made from a 3x4 inch, 4' long oak cants, which would have been cut down to make flooring at the mill, as well as mason jars, and more straight rods. He stained the wood with vinegar that had steel wool sitting in it for a while and finished it off with a sealant. After making the wall sconces for the living room, stairwell, and upstairs hall in a similar fashion, we ended up with the most unique, beautiful lighting for a fraction of the cost it would have taken to purchase similar pieces. Now that the wood plant has closed down for good, the light fixtures and furniture made from materials they provided are even more special. By day Glen worked as the supervisor there, by night he worked on these projects for our house.

In May, I also fixed up a couple of our old garden boxes and started 20 varieties of herbs, the on-demand water heater arrived, Glen installed trim board on all four corners of the house and filled the attic with insulation and the kids played with their cousins in the front yard. I decluttered the camper, preparing to empty it by the 7th, and while I made a huge batch of sunscreen, Glen sat on the staging by the gable end of the porch, applying scalloped board and baton and painting it purple, with Atlas sitting beside him.

In spite of the constant busyness at home, and the time crunch we put ourselves under, we accepted opportunities to help others with joy. Our friends were preparing to disconnect their RV from their house for good, so we paid a visit and Glen helped them rewire their electrical system. It was so synchronistic – they disconnecting from their house to embark on their RV adventure, and we, disconnecting from our camper, to complete ours.

Near the end of May, I posted a photo of a pile of laundry on the bed in the camper. "Glen is concocting a gravity-fed, pump-run combination water system for our house," I wrote. "While I am trying to keep children in bed and tackling laundry and dishes. He working on our new home, me keeping things tied down in our old home. This is how we be rollin' till it's done. Partners in crime, supporting each other in the best ways we can." May 29th, the first piece of drywall in the house was installed on the girls' bedroom ceiling.

The sheetrocking had begun and continued in earnest as if it was going out of style. Meanwhile, we had two more young cousins over for a sleepover, a baby bird hatched in the nest over the screenhouse door and Glen stopped hanging sheetrock long enough to install real outlets and light switches as we went from one room to the next.

I can still picture him in my mind, standing by the bedroom window in the boys' room that faces the front yard, holding a sheet of sheetrock with his knee against the wall, bracing it with his left forearm, while he pushed from over his head with his right arm, elbow wrapped tightly in athletic gauze under his sweatshirt, as he screwed the sheet to the framing.

"This man. Words… How can I explain my heart," I posted. "This man, who works a full day, managing a woodworking plant then comes home to play with his children, eat dinner with his family, and then takes a 15-minute nap to rest his hurting joints before spending another 4-5 hours building our home, finally going to bed after 11 pm, only to do it all again the next day… every day now. He won't rest now until we're all sleeping under this roof. This man, who doesn't complain, says he's just providing for his family but takes the time to tend to details to make this home the best there is. This man, who still finds time to tickle and tease his kids, and ask them how their day went. And the only thing he asks for? My company. So he's not alone when he's working on the house at night. He's pretty amazing."

On June 8th, the day Glen finished sheetrocking the upstairs and moved to the living room, I finally conceded to the growing concept in my mind of this book. I wasn't ready to face the emotional challenges behind it, but I verbally recognized that my last book, A Year In a Camper, was now incomplete and needed a sequel. I bought a notebook and started laying out an outline.

In the small moments I could squeeze out, I continued work on my fledgling herbal business, and began contemplating the idea of going to school to become a master herbalist. Glen had his concerns about the time commitment but suggested that we budget it out. We may both have been utterly exhausted but seeing all the progress on the house was motivating in other areas of our lives.

On the morning of the last day of school, after yet another late night in the house, I picked up a large, bold coffee with espresso. Glen responded to my photo with one of himself, fake sleeping at a picnic table at work, a mug of coffee in hand, and napkin full of Cheezelts in front of his face. People laughed at our back and forth on Facebook, but I think they understood what it represented. That night Glen hung up the light fixtures in the kitchen and dining room, and I captioned them, "hello, new home. We've been waiting a long time to meet you."

The first couple days of summer vacation were spent wrapping up loose ends, and then I faced the first bedroom wall with a mud tray in one hand and spatula in the other. I had three weeks to do the upstairs, and I was already wiped. But damn it, those bedrooms were going to be done and we were going to move in! By day I mudded and sanded, and at night I would treat Glen's elbow with herbs and re-wrap it.

Parenting escapades continued, and mama guilt raged. Someone spilled motor oil in the van, causing me to stop my work long enough to clean it up. I wanted so bad to be more accessible to them. Ten-year-old Nemo was in charge of lunches. They didn't have tablets yet, but there was a lot of access to TV and movies. One day, I did stop long enough to plant herb starters in the garden with Atlas and Amelia. I still remember the little gasps of awe and the tender way they held the little plants as they inspected the roots and little greens. It was magic in the midst of chaos.

Glen began building the dorm room-style bunk beds, with bed on top and desk on the bottom, one for each child, and I started prepping for our camping-themed joint birthday party for the kids on the last Saturday of June, with s'more kits in mini hobo bags, snacks made of "cheese-curl flames," "chocolate bear poop," "pretzel twigs," and of course five batches of cupcakes made to look like logs. Family brought kites and balloons, we had fun games to play, and the kids received gifts that could be used in their new bedrooms, including spending money that got them curtains and desk lamps.

"Partying over by 6 pm, the visiting by 11 pm, we cleaned up child puke from too much partying at 12:15, back to bed at 1 am, slept a whole 8 hours (the first since school got out!), the campers are packing up, and now we can clean up from the mess, but we survived the first big event of the summer."

The kids picked the colors they wanted for their rooms, and

we positioned lines down the middle of each bedroom, so each child had half a room with their chosen paint color. Nemo chose a flat gray, Atlas chose a soft green, Daphney a baby purple, and Amelia chose pumpkin orange. Each one reflected their personalities and interests perfectly.

June 28th, our most popular YouTube video: "Cheap RV Woodstove $200" broke 100,000 views. Even though we weren't adding new videos to our channel, it seemed perfect that such a momentous thing would happen right then. I wrote: "One more week. I cannot speak for Glen, but I am exhausted. I haven't felt my muscles this worked since I volunteered at [a farm] when I was 14. It really makes you relish every break. But we have to keep going. The end is so damn close. Next week we'll be sleeping in our new beds, and then I can rest a little. No, the house won't be finished, but the kids' rooms will be, and aside from mudding, plumbing, and some finish work, the rest of the house will be too. We're really hoping to be entirely in by Thanksgiving. But truly our hearts and minds are already moving. Next week it will be our home. Just hang in their body, we got this!" Friends and family enjoyed all the photo updates, and sent messages like, "cheering you guys on to the finish line! You guys are amazing!"

I am so grateful for the stories and feelings I captured at the moment because so much of it gets lost or tangled over time. The emotions behind stories as they happened are more perfectly understood in entries like this one on June 30th: "It's hard to explain why these children's bedrooms are so monumental to us. Yes, we are building the house ourselves, yes we are done living in our temporary home, but these rooms, these rooms are special. Nemo, who was four when we moved out of "our old house," never slept in a finished room. We left it under construction. Atlas doesn't remember living in a house, and Daphney hardly. Amelia has never lived in a house, period. These bedrooms will just be regular old bedrooms to most people. Yes, we chose the hard road for the greater goal, and we will absolutely treasure every bit of this home, but our kids cannot wait to have bedrooms to call their own. And we, who could not provide them with "the perfect nursery" when they started out on their own journeys, cannot wait to give them this gift. Yes, this is a monumental moment in our lives. Seven days."

The clouds grew dark and ominous. We gathered with neighbors at the top of the hill to watch the skies over the valley. They had predicted thunderstorms and tornadoes across the state, and the rare tornado warning was always sure to draw onlookers in our corner of the country. The kids sat in the van until they felt safe enough to venture out and get a better look, but sadly, nothing exciting did we see. We returned home and Glen installed doors on our bedroom and the bathroom. Our first bedroom door in six years.

Do you remember the scene in The Dark Knight where Joker blows up the hospital? There is a popular meme from that moment where he walks away from the hospital, it blows up, and he turns around and shakes his head. The meme reads, "when I turn my back on my kids for a minute." This is how I was feeling in those last days.

It was like they knew they could get away with murder because there was no one to watch them. After starting the painting of their rooms together, we participated in an Independence Day parade with Glen's family and then dropped the kids off at my mom and stepdad's for three days. I was so relieved because even though I would miss them terribly, I knew they were finally getting the attention they needed, and I knew that when they returned it would be done. Visions of them walking into their completed rooms gave me a boost of energy to push through to the end.

We had been working toward this for so long, that it hardly felt real. Was this really happening? The day after they left, I washed the mudding tools in a five-gallon pail filled from the rain barrel out front, and a good friend kept me company as I processed the emotions of cleaning the kids' bedroom in the camper for the last time. The day was completed, however, in perhaps the most emotional moment of the day, when I made our master bed in the house that night. For six years I had been climbing over a mattress on the floor to cram the edges of the blanket between the mattress and the wall in our tiny room, and here I was, walking all the way around the sides of the bed, our four-poster bed, to smooth out the comforter and fluff the pillows. It was the most amazing moment, and my heart burst with joy and gratitude. Glen and I moved in that night.

The day before picking up the kids was the most fun. Glen assembled the stools he made for the kids' desks, which he laser-engraved with their names at the mill, and I organized their rooms: hanging up the curtains, their artwork, and setting out their personal belongings on shelves and their desks. I couldn't wait for them to come home the next day, and I was sure that once they entered their rooms, they wouldn't come out for days!

July 7th. I sat on the porch steps, and before I could hear the car, I knew they were coming when I heard screams of "the house!" as my mom drove up the driveway. The kids poured out of the car and ran screaming and giggling up the steps. It was the best Christmas morning ever. How my mom managed to contain the excitement long enough to take the kids swimming at the ocean before dropping them off, I don't know, but the kids came home wrapped in beach towels, and they sat on the porch squealing in glee, screaming, "we have a house!" as I captured their first moments on video. They left with their home being in the camper and returned to walk into their home, in a house.

My mom and I followed them upstairs as they ran from room to room, checking everything out, climbing up into their beds, and screaming out celebration they could not contain. Nemo stood in the doorway, dropped his bag and jaw, and just stood there staring at his side of the room for what seemed like forever. Daphney just wouldn't stop screaming, and climbed up in her bed and bounced around, giggling and yelling. Atlas and Amelia were slightly quieter, but not much. They wanted to check out everything in their rooms and were excited to see all their toys, including some that had been lost under their camper beds for a while. My mom cried, the camera recorded, and the memory ingrained itself as a turning point in the history of our family. This. This is what it was all for.

When Glen came home, the kids wanted to show him their spaces right away. Nemo was owning his space by putting up his drawings, and the others were busy playing and reorganizing.

Glen was right. Since we had spent so much time in the house already, and he and I had already spent two nights in our new bed, it didn't feel quite so climactic when I returned from brushing my teeth in the camper that night and closed the door behind me. Just like that, we were home.

Our house design is really quite simple. It is 16' by 32', two stories tall, with a one-pitch roof facing the front, North-West side of the house, and our large front yard. The back faces big power lines and the woods.

The master bedroom, single shared bathroom, and small pantry are downstairs, along with an open room that includes the kitchen, dining room, and living room. Because it is not very big, it really feels like one room only suggested to be separated by flooring types, lighting, and furniture.

Stairs in the back, far corner, beside the pantry, lead upstairs to the long hall where two doors lead to the girls' and boys' rooms. The girls' room also holds the "water closet," which instead of being a second bathroom, contains three 55-gallon barrels of water and a pump. Our rainwater is drained down the gutters into 260-gallon tanks, pumped into more tanks in the ¾, ledge-covered basement, and then pumped to the barrels upstairs, where it can either be pumped down or gravity-fed to the faucets.

We have big windows, big enough that higher than standard ceilings were required to meet code. Extra insulation fills exterior walls, the crawlspace under the roof, the ceiling between the boys' room and master bedroom, and most of the basement ceiling. The basement is accessed through an opening in the extra-large foundation footer. Between insulation and windows, it is rarely an uncomfortable temperature in the summer and holds heat well in the winter. The wood stove provides more than enough heat, and we keep a shade in the stairwell to keep the upstairs from getting too hot.

Everything in the house was chosen specifically for its design and features, from the single-hung windows to the unique, homemade lighting fixtures, to the repurposed wood for shelving, and the décor with family significance. It's a unique home, it gets lots of compliments from guests, and we love it.

"Three days ago our family moved into our house. There were times in the past six years when I honestly wondered if this would ever happen. We chose to live in a camper because we wanted to take a bad situation and turn it into something good. Something very good. The road has had its ups and downs. These ups and downs were more extreme than I could ever have anticipated. The joys we have experienced so far are hard to explain but need to be felt personally in order to truly understand. The hardships have been just shy of gut-wrenching. And they too are near-impossible to put into words. Words that can be felt. The ache for this, the longing, will we ever succeed? Can we actually, actually do this? I could only hold on to hope and keep pushing, keep pushing, trust that it will work out. I shared the following poem months back, in the last of my deep lows, in which I felt like a caged mother animal, unable to care for my young on the other side of the bars. I knew we would be free. I could see the evidence sitting before me, but damn does it feel... so incredibly relieving to be on the other side. Appreciation for things can only truly be felt on the other side of hardship. Every. Single. Little. Thing we have in this house so far, everything is a blessing. Yes, we've worked our butts off, shed tears and real blood and pain earning the money and building it. But as I sit here (in my house!) I wonder how we managed to be on the receiving end of all this goodness. We own it. No bank has the rights to it. It's ours as long as we want it to be. And it's beautiful, and it's perfect, and I can see God's love in the details that have come through in ways we could not have planned. This was destined to be a good summer, of hope fulfilled, but now I understand. The waiting did make sense. And I am literally crying while writing this because even though the work is far from done, our worries are over, and we are okay, and we are right where we need, and want to be. And I cannot express how blessed and happy I am to be in this moment, right here."

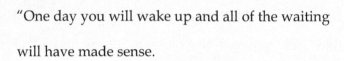

"One day you will wake up and all of the waiting

will have made sense.

You will realize that all of the prayers

that seemed to be tangled in worries

were actually wrapped tightly in God's grace.

You will realize that even though before

you were certain it was over, you were actually

okay, and everything that was supposed to happened

happened and you are right where you

need to be."

~ Morgan Harpor Nichols

The next few days were busy but had a different energy to them. I had always thought that I would prefer to wait to move in until every little thing was done, but now, instead of rushing like crazy people to get things done, we could pick away at jobs and enjoy the house at the same time. We still had a big empty room for a kitchen and living area with not even a sheet of drywall, but with a touch of TLC, it was cozy enough.

The day after we moved in, Nemo's train collection moved from storage to his bedroom, and his area was complete. On one side of the living area was a table piled high with chop saw, hand tools, nails, and other construction supplies; on the other was the table moved from the camper, holding a camp stove and other simple cooking supplies. The camper was renamed; the tin can became the mess hall where we baked food and washed dishes and the locker room where we showered and brushed teeth.

A trip to the lumber yard provided us with pine for bedroom shelving, pantry shelving, and a generous gift of nice plywood that Glen would later use for raised panels throughout the house. That night we reused thin strips of wood from another project to build wooden crates for our wardrobe. I cut the wood with the chop saw on the porch, and he nailed them together inside. The kids enjoyed playing in the pile of sawdust left in front of the main entrance from miscellaneous projects.

Within a couple of days, our master bedroom wardrobe was complete: an open-style system I found inspiration for on Pinterest with room to hang clothes on the sides and shelves above, below, and in the center. He finished off the nightstands he built and laser-engraved with "Mama" and "Papa." Every day there was some new thing to experience and enjoy. It was like Christmas every day and the more we created our space, the more energy we had to keep creating. We hung a hammock in our bedroom and I sat down with a kiddo in my lap to read with them. Christmas every day.

Lots of sorting, organizing, and cleaning followed. Glen built the pantry, and gradually, more and more belongings were moved from the camper to the house. He connected an antenna to the TV in the living room, and for the first time in years, we were able to watch a movie or TV show without sitting on a bed.

I hung up a large, cross-stitched piece of our wedding above our bed, and other artwork was hung with love, while Glen started up on the raised panels. We fell into a new rhythm; him building, me cleaning, and organizing. By the end of the month, I had cleaned enough to host my first party – a boho jewelry show. The creator displayed her work on the long dresser in the living room that would find it's way to the boys' room a few days later. It had been a gift from friends. The girls inherited a large dresser from my parents that they had given to us before our move to the land and had been storing for us. This was a big change from the plastic totes they had been using in the camper to keep their clothes condensation free!

Simple things like a trash can frequently brought smiles to my face. After hanging grocery bags on a doorknob as a trash can for six years, a full-sized trash can becomes a gift. We also enjoyed opening the windows on both sides of the house and letting the breeze blow through that summer. To not be stuck inside the camper, where the temperature would easily soar to 100 degrees was a relief to us all, and no one complained about the heat that summer!

The kids continued their outdoor play as always. As much as they loved their new rooms, nothing could keep them inside for long! One day, Atlas strapped a wind-up radio to his belt, plugged in his headphones, headed outside barefoot, and "seedwacked" as he would say, with the new battery-operated weed wacker he had earned for extra reading work. It was his favorite possession for a long time!

The herbs in the garden grew, along with my herbal consulting business, but we made a difficult decision to re-home our chickens. Our favorite rooster and hen had been killed earlier in the spring, we weren't getting any eggs from the older hens, and we were faced with the decision of getting more or rehousing them. Somehow it just seemed like the right time to say goodbye to chicken-raising for a while. So the rooster went to the soup pot and the last five hens joined a friend's brood. "No more hens begging for food at our door... or pooping on the doorstep. No more roosters chasing kids... or entertaining us with their personalities. No more trudging through the snow in the dark to tend to birds... or enjoying watching them bathe in the hot sun. Mixed feelings – relief, yet sadness. It's a good change, and it's the right thing for us all, but the memories make it bittersweet."

By the end of July, more siding had been done, the kitchen island had been built, the hutch had been rebuilt and painted, we received a housewarming gift of our first plant, and we had our first friend sleepover. Construction continued, but life was slowing down a tad and beginning to look a little more normal.

Everyone had their favorite place in the house. Mine was our bedroom. Shortly before we moved, I had a nightmare that mice were crawling all over us. Mice were a never-ending battle to fight, and then there was the mold, not to mention being cramped, having the dirty laundry hamper by the head of my bed, and having tiny windows to let in light. I loved that my new room had beautiful big windows, was dry, clean, and though small, it felt spacious.

"Our bedroom. It has a long way to go before we're done. Mudding, painting, curtains. Flooring, desk, guitars in their proper place. But I am happy. When I was a young teen, I volunteered at a health center and farm, overseen by this amazing lady, and it was my peaceful escape from a crazy time in my life. They say you should create a peaceful place to visualize in times of distress, but I didn't need to because it existed in real life! At this place, filled with bedrooms, parlors, kitchen, farmer's porches, gardens, etc. peace was the residing guest. There was minimal technology, hidden for occasional use, but rarely taken out, food was always cooking, flowers abounding in warmth, singing together in the living room took over their jobs in the cold. The bedrooms were places of pure rest, with minimal objects to distract, but beautiful beds, chairs, rugs, and paintings. The kitchen was always abuzz, and guests would stop to chat and smile. The porches and gardens were the places to be if you wanted entertainment (or rest after an honest day's work!). This place was where you could go to be together with others who cared about simple beauty, true peace, and good health. As we create our home, images keep coming back to me of this place. I don't need to recreate it, but the feeling of the place is something I want to live here. So as we unpack, I know what it feels like to be in a place where there is a place for everything, and minimal excess – everything has a useful or beautiful purpose – and I want to protect that. Our bedroom will be a place to retreat to. It will be a place for peaceful rest. I'm not even sure I want a TV in there, as originally planned. I love leaving the windows open at night and waking up to the song of birds, and of having a better view through the windows. I love having more blank wall space and only things I really want in there, instead of it being a place to store things, like before. And I hope that I can help the rest of our home to feel the same way as it comes into its own."

I miss the sound of the rain. You could hear it coming through the thin walls, and then all of a sudden it was pounding on the ceiling and those plastic vents that lined the hall. Sometimes it was gentle and relaxing, and other times a deafening noise that woke sleeping children. That sound may have heralded thoughts of mold growing in the moisture left behind or warned of wind coming up the valley, but still, I found it reassuring. In all it's glory and rough edges, the wild weather was predictable and trustworthy. It could lay ruin in its wake, or lull us to sleep at night, but nature and we had become friends.

When we moved into the house, the well-insulated walls and windows blocked out the sounds of our friend, the wild. I remember standing in front of a window, watching it pour and not being able to hear anything and thinking, "this is wrong. I feel numbed. I'm not connected." And proceeded to open the window as wide as I dared so I could be a part of it again. To this day, when there is rain, I have to open the window to listen, and one of my favorite things is sleeping with my head exposed to the full moon's light, curtains drawn back, and light pouring in. I have similar feelings about hearing the birds chirping in the early morning and have always enjoyed being connected to the earth's cycles, but living in the camper, so close to nature for several years, gave me more respect and admiration for God's handiwork. That's why the window by my bed is my favorite spot.

However close we wish to be to the outdoors, no matter how much we feel comfortable, connected to its cycles and sounds, the wind is one thing that has changed us on this journey. After the porch blew over in 2013, with my husband in it, our visceral reaction to the wind has never been the same. Even though logically I know we'll be okay if the wind is blowing when I fall asleep, I have to remind myself that the house is not going to blow over, and we will be okay, even as my heart races and visions of destruction fill my head. On such nights, Glen will sleep with noise canceling headphones on. We've learned to live in awe and connection with nature, and at the same time with a strong respect for its power.

We knew that we would be spending the third week of August at camp as usual, but that didn't slow us down. True to character, it put a fire under our butts to see how much more we could get done! In addition to planning the first quarter of school for my class the coming year, and volunteering in kids church, I hosted and taught a doTERRA class, and moved stuff in and out of the kitchen as Glen worked on it.

Using wood from his childhood home's barn and apple crates from an orchard next door, he created beautiful cupboard doors for the island, upper cabinets, and a sink cabinet. He also got his hands on more 2 ½" oak cants at work, and with $50 worth of glue and apoxie, he made a beautiful countertop for the island, with a bar top finish. Just before leaving, we tag-teamed the kitchen tile: he applied and grouted, and I followed behind to wash them. Technically, we were supposed to be off the tile for a couple of days to let it harden appropriately, and leaving it untouched while at camp was the perfect timing; if we could just get it done in time! Amelia remembers being forbidden from walking on the tile. Because it covered the entryway, the kids came in and out of the house via a ladder out the back door. It was very close to the stairs leading to the bedrooms, so unless they had a reason to go upstairs, they stayed outdoors to play until bedtime. Food was served outside at the picnic table and they used the outhouse when they needed to use the bathroom. The night before we left it was finally complete, and we started packing camp gear so we could leave in the morning.

Camp was a much-needed reprieve, and was filled with swimming, making friends, a birthday party, nature walks, and reading. Glen and Atlas both needed camp to rest their sore bodies; Glen his shoulder and elbow, Atlas his knee, and it would be almost two weeks before Glen was back on the staging, putting siding up on one side of the house. By the end of August, we hardly used the camper at all, and we were getting anxious to bid it good riddance.

"Seven weeks ago we moved into our home. In that time, many improvements have been made, but it continues to be a work in progress. The dishes I just washed in the camper kitchen are waiting on the house table to be put away, a washing routine that will likely continue a while longer. But I don't mind a bit. We may have to use the camper for baths and dishes through the fall, but we're still living in our house. And I am grateful to be in this season of limbo and inconvenience because it's the next step. This winter will be hard. We could be using a cooler for a fridge, heating water on the stove for dishes, and bathing in a tub with water heated on the stove, but it's all good, cause we're in our house."

Chapter Nine

~Finishing Strong~

There is a certain moment in time where you realize you have made an emotional connection to the home you live in. It's that moment you know you are home and you belong there. For me, I didn't recognize that feeling until I left our homes for a short time and felt satisfied in our return. We went to camp for a week in August 2012, and when we returned, our camper felt like an old friend. We returned from the same camp in August 2017, and that same satisfaction flooded our hearts, but this time, in our house. We were home.

We continued to fill weekends and vacations with house projects after moving in. Over Christmas vacation, I mudded and sanded our master bedroom twice, and during February vacation, I painted, Glen put up trim, I hung curtains, and he built a desk shortly after. We regularly went through waves of activity: some weeks found us working our tails off, and other weeks, nothing changed in the house at all. We rode the waves as they came and enjoyed the changes as they developed.

In the midst of these early months, Glen's work situation changed. The company he worked for closed, and he spent five weeks building forms for bridge sections, before being hired back by the construction company he was laid off from in 2010, as a carpenter and job site supervisor. Interesting how it all came full circle. These transitions were difficult but being in the house made it easier and less depressing to weather them.

Right before Glen stopped working at the plant, as projects were wrapped up, he was given permission to turn unclaimed wood into furniture for our house. In the days prior to the closure, he spent all spare minutes, break times, and after-hours quickly planning, cutting, sanding, and moving prepared pieces back home, where he assembled our dining room table with bench seats, our first couch, a coffee table, and a countertop out of beautiful oak. He was exhausted, but he built furniture worth thousands for pennies on the dollar and did a wonderful job.

That same winter, from 2017-2018, our camper appliances were moved into the house, and we set up a new wash routine that would take us through the next year when Glen built a beautiful rock shower, and finished connecting the wastewater pipes to the gray water leach field in the fall of 2018. For the first year, water was pumped through the faucets but was drained into buckets that we emptied outside, and our shower consisted of a horse trough with a shower curtain tacked to the wall around it, the camper shower head, and a 12-volt pump with a hose to drain it out the window when we were done.

In early spring, after our first winter in our house and the master bedroom was done, doors were hung in the kids' rooms and painting happened in the conjoined living room and dining room; Benton Harbor blue. I wrote in a rather exasperated moment, "always in the middle, never at the end." These home projects continued to fill in spare moments during school vacations and weekends.

We celebrated making it through our first winter since 2011 on only the water we had stored in the basement, all 1,000 gallons, and drinking water we trucked in. With a little help from storm lanterns and tarps reducing the space to heat in the basement, it stayed largely unfrozen the whole winter.

Less work was done in the summer of 2018, as we tried to rest and spend more time together with the kids, but the urgency of winter brought on another wave of activity in the fall. Changes were made to the plumbing, and the shower was built from Pennsylvania fieldstone, strategically placed rock treasures the kids had given us, a showerhead Glen built from a copper bucket he found in his childhood barn, and intentionally aged copper piping. He also built a stone wall behind our newly installed woodstove and assembled the metal chimney on the exterior wall. That winter we heated partially on kerosene as before, and partially on wood.

In 2019, we nearly finished designing our bathroom; finally installing sheetrock, a pedestal sink, a urinal Glen made from an old fire extinguisher, a wood-paneled accent wall (which doubled as hidden access to the pipes), and a tile floor. We painted the walls bright orange and the wood paneling gray. We would be stuck with the bucket-compost toilet for a while longer.

Also, that year, we painted the living room ceiling, the pantry, and the stairway. Glen installed pine treads on the stairs and stained them dark brown; installed vents in the attic and cleared out the mold that had been growing without them.

This year, 2020, has been an eventful year thus far, as it has been for most people around the world. We anticipate that projects will continue, but our roots are digging even deeper, and we even brought home our first indoor pet, a kitty named Wilbur. On the house this year, we have installed the new electric fridge and propane cook stove, made a new cement countertop with under mount for the sink, applied stone to the wall behind the fridge and stove, built a hood for the stove out of a bourbon barrel, and outside, have begun the stonework on the front of the house. Using a delivery of "riff-raff" stone, Glen is building stone onto prepared walls around the porch, up to railing height, and down the stairs. It will create a beautiful walkway, and also cover up the unsightly tall basement walls. Finally, Glen built a wall in the basement to better support the main floor and provide support for new shelving, and built a temporary, but much safer power house for our generators, batteries, inverter, converter, and monitors.

We recently estimated that altogether, we have spent at minimum $50,000 on our house, possibly closer to $60,000. We continue to purchase all materials with cash and as time allows, and anticipate being completely finished in another couple of years. Altogether, this cash-built house will easily be a ten year project!

One of the most unexpected things that came from this lifestyle, both while living in the camper and afterwards was the difficulty I had in spending money and time on things I defined as frivolous; things that didn't propel our building project forward. Anytime we spent money on a day trip, it was money not invested in the house. As much as I wanted to redirect my energy, living seven years with one agenda had left its mark. With time, each act of defiance toward my ingrained response made it easier and easier, and I felt it a victory to see that, at the time of this writing, we have set aside several thousand dollars for a five-week road trip together. We had hoped to go this year, but due to the pandemic, we will have to wait another year. This, even though we still need decks finished, flooring, a permanent compost toilet, and proper propane piping connections, as well as a power house for the solar setup, the stonework and landscaping complete, trim work finished, and painting in the hall complete, I am excited to be redirecting our finances toward investment in our family because we can.

Recently, I was interviewed for Renee's podcast, the same Renee who went on a thru-hiking trip with her family. On her podcast, we talked about all things home. In the midst of the conversation, she made a comment about finishing. She said, "you did it. You finished what you set out to do." Yes. We did that. Some days it's hard to believe that it all worked out, but it did! And we are so thankful and proud. At some point, I wrote in my journal this quote: "I want to inspire people. I want someone to look at me and say, because of you, I didn't give up." I didn't do this for other people, but I have to say that an overriding theme for both Glen and I through this process has been finding purpose in encouraging others who want to start fresh in similar situations. We may be the bearers of bad news when it comes to the realities of such a lifestyle, but if they are convinced it's what they're going to do, we have hoped that our stories can be of help as they find their way.

We were so anxious to leave this stage of our lives behind us. During the building process, some would reach out for support in reaching their dreams, or implementation of plans to move into campers or cabins, because they had been watching and we, through our online presence, gave them hope that they could do it too. I would grit my teeth and force a smile because even though the sacrifices we made are absolutely worth the prize, it's like asking a mother who is still pushing her baby out whether she thinks you should have a baby. No matter how much she loves being pregnant or having babies in her home, at that moment she's apt to answer with a growl and utter a few explicit words. And because off-grid and tiny homes are highly glorified at the moment, it's hard for anyone to understand how these situations are remotely similar, unless you have experienced it yourself.

And yet, behind those dreams they express to us, I see myself ten years ago, frustrated with the failings of the American dream, wanting to start fresh, with no one dictating how we design our lives. I hear the yearning of their heart's desire for simplicity; I see the joy in their eyes as they speak of untethering themselves from modern constraints. I recognize that look, that excitement because I felt it too. In fact, it's not hard to find people who have also heard this call.

After the climax of birth has passed and the woman is no longer in the thick of "Labor Land," she will be able to highlight the passion and wonder of the experience, and she may even say she'd do it again for the reward. She just has to have time to process the birth emotionally first. Writing this book has been a helpful way for me to process our experience, but up until the past year or so, it was very difficult for me to talk about it without a noticeable undercurrent of frustration. I am able now to see the passion and goodness intertwined with the hardship; the calling people experience, and the desire to step outside of their door in search of adventure. So yes, it was hard. It was a very long, difficult labor of love. But the home birthed out of it, and the growth experience required to fight for the dream, has absolutely been worth it.

It would be interesting, exciting, hard, that much we knew. But was it what we expected? Nothing like it. Ask a woman what giving birth is like and she hesitates. How do you explain something in words that you felt with your whole being?

Moving our family into a camper, living there for six years, making sacrifices that whole time to build a forever home that was sustainable and debt-free? Totally worth it. Do it again? Eh. Maybe not so much. But to explain what it was like is such a difficult task to attempt, one which held me back from writing this book, even throughout the writing of it.

Before the move, I began writing our story, using the excitement and angst to motivate me and help me find the words. After we moved, the desire to express our vision on paper waned for a time. Instead, I spent the time soaking it in. I didn't pick up the pen again for three months, and similar periods of time later on. I took notice of things most people took for granted; things we had gone without for so long that we truly appreciated having: walking space, the house not rocking when a child jumped, private space, a table big enough for all of us, more reasonable temperatures from day to night. We lived around the construction process and mess, but with grateful and cheerful hearts. Celebrating completed projects on a regular basis, instead of having to wait months to have the weather or money to support a major, but a short-lived phase. Now, a simple thing like another wall sided, a shelf installed, a sink in the house made our hearts lighter, because it could happen more frequently and be completed faster.

We are a DIY-type of family. We thrive on big ideas, creativity, resourcefulness, and challenges to conquer. Tell us something isn't possible, and we'll make a way for it to happen; that's just our thing. Somehow, I thought this experience would be similar. In some ways, it has been, but it's so much more. Living in a small space together has pushed us to the brink of "learn to get along through thick or thin together or sink together." If Glen and I weren't so damn stubborn, didn't have such high principles about the sanctity of marriage and family, and if I hadn't had such a nasty experience with divorce and it's consequences growing up, I can't say that we would have stayed together. But God is good. All the storms we had traveled through in the past had served a greater purpose. And here we are. Together, in a better relationship than we had to begin with.

Living off-grid has also reconstructed every preconceived idea of what it means to be conservative and to be thankful for what we have. Building a home with our own hands and hard-earned money has forced me to draw from strength deep within that only existed out of necessity.

Just as I said earlier, no adventure can be had without trials; no breathtaking views without paying the price. This adventure has cost us far more than I budgeted, but we have been rewarded along the journey in ways I could not have foreseen, and the ultimate view at the top feels so much grander than I had imagined. Just as a thru-hiker or a new mother will never be the same after their journey, the six of us are forever changed. We are stronger, more resilient, wiser, more patient. We are grateful for the little things (even as small as a light switch!), taking nothing for granted. These things we wouldn't have learned without trial.

The little adventures along the way; building alongside our children, lying out under the stars, marshmallows over the fire, trees to climb, sliding down the icy hill, and the process of making the house our own; designing it, building it, paying for it, enjoying it. It has been far more thrilling than buying our first house and remodeling it was. That was gratifying in the short term, but in the long term, this was even more so.

Today, we have no mortgage, we are not beholden to anyone, or any job, or any bank, to keep our home. Our home is our own, built with our own blood, sweat, and tears. Because of our short term sacrifice, we have earned what cannot be purchased.

We are free. We are home.

Two years after we moved, a visitor by the name of Rowe arrived in the neighborhood. He was a guest of one of our neighbors, and while he was in town, he stopped in to see our friends who bought the enjoining Rowe acreage and started their off-grid homestead. He shared a story about being one of the last of the Rowe family to live on the land. He spoke of raising food on the border between the two plots, and of his mother's trees and flowers that she cared for in the yard. His stories invoked feelings of nostalgia. It brings no small amount of satisfaction, as a sentimental person, to know that while we aren't Rowes by name, the land has remained in the family for 240 years.

I began this story with a quote from Lord of the Rings, one of my favorite stories, by the infamous J.R.R. Tolkien, so I will bookend it with another, from the Hobbit. When our journey began, we could hardly have anticipated where the road would take us; what mountains we would climb, what depths we would descend, what joys we would find, and lessons we would learn. It was everything like in stories of adventures, and nothing like it at all. I have done my best to share the experience of our adventure, but we have ended where we began: with you living an adventure through another's story. I hope you have gained courage and resolve through our story, to attempt your own adventure, so I will leave you with this provocation from wise Tolkien:

"The world is not in your books and maps; it is out there."

Now that we are home, we are, as Bilbo shared with Frodo, "quite ready for another adventure," and hope to be back on the road as soon as we can be.

Now it's your turn. See you on the road.

Post Script

~What happened to the camper?~

Campers are not meant to be lived in, despite them being used for that purpose all of the time. When we moved out of ours, despite regularly filling joints with silicone caulking, replacing parts as they broke, washing mold off the trim too frequently, and even remodeling parts of it, like the floor and cabinets, it continued to deteriorate faster than we could keep up. Key factors in its demise were water damage, mold, ants, rot, and broken handles, screens, and other small parts. Staying in a camper is intended to be a short-term solution, and between parking it on wet land and overstaying our welcome, it is no longer in any condition to be lived in.

Despite this, before we had even set a date to move out of the camper, we had multiple families asking us about buying the "American Family Now camper." We took it as a compliment and were honored that our camper would mean something to them, but had serious concerns about the health and safety implications of anyone moving in, and discouraged them from buying it. Until we learned that our town would not need to issue us a residency permit for our house, we felt compelled to keep it on our property anyway.

Meanwhile, over the past couple of years, our eldest daughter has developed a surprising love for tiny homes, and she requested that we keep the camper so that when she has saved up the money to rebuild it, we can tear down the trailer to its frame and help her rebuild it according to her design. If her dreams do come to fruition, how beautiful it would be for her to live on top of the foundation that started our lifestyle, and which she lived on for so many years.

About the author

Naomi Kilbreth is a Christian Clinical Herbalist. She lives off grid in rural Maine with her husband and four children, in the home they built themselves. She has authored two other books: Inspired Birth: A Fresh Perspective on Childbirth for Christian Maternity Care Providers, and A Year In a Camper: A Family's Story of Rediscovering the American Dream, both available on Amazon. You can learn more about Naomi and her work by visiting www.laureltreewellnessLLC.com.

Made in the USA
Middletown, DE
08 July 2022